A Practitioner's Guide to Public Relations Research, Measurement, and Evaluation

A Practitioner's Guide to Public Relations Research, Measurement, and Evaluation

Don W. Stacks and David Michaelson

A Practitioner's Guide to Public Relations Research,
Measurement, and Evaluation

First published in 2010 by
Business Expert Press, LLC
222 East 46th Street, New York, NY 10017
www.businessexpertpress.com

ISBN-13: 978-1-60649-101-0 (paperback)
ISBN-10: 1-60649-101-6 (paperback)

ISBN-13: 978-1-60649-102-7 (e-book)
ISBN-10: 1-60649-102-4 (e-book)

DOI 10.4128/9781606491027

A publication in the Business Expert Press Public Relations collection

Collection ISSN: Forthcoming (print)
Collection ISSN: Forthcoming (electronic)

Cover design by Jonathan Pennell
Interior design by Scribe, Inc.

First edition: May 2010

10 9 8 7 6 5 4 3 2 1

Printed in the United States of America.

For our Robins . . . and Katie, Jonathan,
Meg, Stacy, Caroline, and George

Abstract

This volume introduces the reader to the world of research and public relations research in particular. It takes a best practices approach—one that focuses on taking the appropriate method and rigorously applying that method to collect the data that best answer the objectives of the research. It also presents an approach to public relations that focuses on establishing the profession's impact on the client's return on investment in the public relations function, whether that function be aimed at internal or external audiences. By the end of the book, the reader will not be a research expert but will understand why and how research is conducted. Further, the reader will be able to apply best practice standards to any research done by supply side vendors or internal research departments.

Keywords

Research, public relations, best practice(s), research methods, statistical analysis, goals and objectives, secondary research, content analysis, survey and poll research, experimentation, content analysis, return on investment (ROI), return on expectation (ROE), sampling, focus groups, interviewing, qualitative research, quantitative research, measurement, evaluation, nonfinancial indicators, media analysis

Contents

Preface

Over the past several decades, the world has changed dramatically. When we both started our work in public relations research and education, word processors and computers were just being introduced to the workplace, the Internet was merely a concept, the cell phone was an extravagant luxury only available to the wealthy, Twitter and blogging were not part of the vernacular, and the fax machine was the "latest and greatest" technology. While much has changed in the practice of public relations since the 1970s because of these advances, the principles, methods, and skills associated with solid research remain constant, with measurement and evaluation continuing as the foundation for creating effective public relations programs.

In an environment where everyone has ready access to the same basic research tools, the challenge today is building a solid foundation of fundamental research skills based on best practices. What distinguishes this book from other treatises on research is our unique perspective based on our positions as a public relations educator and a public relations research practitioner. This perspective combines the rigor of academic thinking with the practical application of conducting research to improve the day-to-day practice of public relations.

This book was written for the reader who wants to know more about how and why research can add to what we know about public relations and the effects of public relations practices as they relate to business outcomes. It is different in that its focus is on the best practices that lead to the gathering of data appropriate for the reason the research is being conducted—it leads to an understanding of (1) what research methods should be employed, (2) why those research methods will yield the most appropriate data, and (3) how these data should be evaluated. It assumes that the reader has little or no real practice in public relations research but wants to better understand and possibly conduct such research.

This book covers a wide variety of topics exploring each of the essential best practices, ranging from setting research objectives to conducting content analysis to analyzing survey data. However, it is not a textbook. Nor is it a manual. Rather, it is a treatise on the value of research and how to ensure that research fulfills its fundamental role as a core of the public relations discipline.

Don W. Stacks
University of Miami
Coral Gables, FL

David Michaelson
Echo Research, Inc.
New York, NY

PART I

Introduction to Public Relations Research, Measurement, and Evaluation

Part I introduces the reader to the practice of public relations and the concept of "best practices." Chapter 1 provides a quick glance at the history of *contemporary* public relations practice and how a best practices approach makes public relations results important to a company or client. Chapter 2 lays out the role of public relations as a necessary requirement in the business world and establishes the groundwork for public relations research—research that focuses on business goals and objectives and the stating of such public relations goals and objectives that are measurable and indicative (can be correlated with) of business' investment in public relations through *return on investment* (ROI). It also introduces the reader to public relations' outcomes and what is labeled *return on expectations* (ROE). Finally, chapter 3 introduces the concept of measurement, assessment, and evaluation of public relations through a coordinated campaign aimed at measuring predispositions toward behavior through attitude, belief, and value measures.

CHAPTER 1

Introduction to Research and Evaluation in Public Relations

Contemporary public relations practice has developed since the mid-20th century from the weak third sister in the marketing, advertising, and public relations mix to gain status as a full and equal player in the corporate suite. Part of that development can be traced to a change in the way public relations is practiced. The early days of public relations functions—limited to media relations and "press agentry"—have evolved into a sophisticated array of communications where public relations is no longer an afterthought, but is an integral part of the communications mix.

A central reason for this change in the perceptions of and stature of public relations in the communications world is the inclusion of research, measurement, and evaluation as a core part of the practice—tools that have been integral to the practice of marketing and advertising for decades. The purpose of this book is to provide the business reader and communications professional with the necessary and practical understanding of the problems and promises of public relations research, measurement, and evaluation—and more importantly, to act as a guide to the effective use of methods, measures, and analysis in providing grounded evidence of the success (or failure) of public relations campaigns.

Defining Public Relations and Its Objectives

What exactly is this profession called public relations? For many it is simply one of three promotional areas that management uses to get its message out: marketing, advertising, and public relations. What has differentiated them in the past can be viewed in terms of (a) what a business expects it to do and (b) the kinds of outcomes it produces. In too many eyes, public relations only includes dealing with *media relations*. That is, the objective of public relations to get coverage of the business—preferably positive—through the "placement" of articles and the like as endorsed by journalists.

But public relations is much more than "press agentry" or media relations. It is better seen as an umbrella term for any number of departments in a business or corporation that seeks to get its messages out to various publics or audiences by managing the flow of information between an *organization* and its *publics* or audiences.[1]

A *public* is a part of a population that has been selected for study; an *audience* is a specifically targeted group within that public that has been targeted for a company's messages. What then is public relations? First and foremost, public relations serves to manage the credibility, reputation, trust, relationship, and confidence of the general public in relation to the company.[2] As Professor Donald K. Wright noted, "Public relations is the management function that identifies, establishes, and maintains mutually beneficial relationships between an organization and the various publics on which its success or failure depends."[3]

How is public relations practiced if it is an umbrella concept? Its practice can be defined by its function in the organization. Public relations takes on the following functions, sometimes alone and at other times as a combined function. The following list is neither complete nor is it by importance of function:

- Community relations
- Corporate communications
- Customer relations
- Employee relations
- Financial relations
- Government relations
- Media relations
- Public affairs
- Strategic communications

What then are public relations' objectives? There three major objectives any public relations campaign seeks to accomplish: (a) to ensure that the

messages get out to their intended audiences and that they are understood ("informational objective"); (b) to monitor the campaign so that
benchmarks regarding the acceptance of messages by target audiences in
terms of cognitive, affective, and behavioral attitudinal or belief acceptance, rejection, or maintenance ("motivational objective"); and (c) predicting what the target audience will actually do based on the campaign
("behavioral objective"). As Stacks points out, each objective must be met
and then monitored before the next objective can be obtained.[4] In forthcoming chapters we will introduce a number of ideas on how a public
relations campaign should operate. We will look at how traditional public
relations campaigns experienced unintended problems due to a lack of
research and how the failure to establish measurable objectives, baselines,
and benchmarks limits the effectiveness of public relations. More importantly, we will introduce a practical approach to public relations research
that will result in better and more effective communications programs.

A Brief History of Public Relations Research

The formal origins of public relations research can be traced to the
1950s.[5] During that period, a company called Group Attitudes Corporation was acquired by Hill & Knowlton.[6] The primary focus of Group
Attitudes Corporation was to function as a stand-alone yet captive
arm of the parent agency. Its work included research for the Tobacco
Institute,[7] as well as for other Hill & Knowlton clients. The primary
focus of this research, taken from a review of several published reports,
was to assess reaction to communications messages and vehicles using
processes that appear similar to the research methods employed by the
advertising industry during this same period. This industry model was
followed over the next 25 years with the establishment of research arms
at several other public relations agencies. In addition to Hill & Knowlton, the major public relations agencies that have had research departments include Burson-Marsteller (Penn Schoen Berland), Ruder Finn
(Research & Forecasts), Ketchum, Weber Shandwick (KRC), Edelman
(Strategy One), Ogilvy Public Relations, APCO, Golin Harris, and GCI
Group. For the most part, the primary function of these agency-based
research departments was similar to the work initially conducted by

Group Attitudes Corporation. Most of these research departments were created internally, with the notable exception of Penn Schoen Berland, which was acquired by WPP and later merged into Burson-Marsteller.

As early as the 1930s, methods were also being developed by advertisers and their agencies that linked exposure and persuasion measures to actual store sales. In essence, testing, measurement, analysis, and evaluation systems became an integral part of the advertising industry. These systems became so institutionalized by mid-decade that an academic journal—*The Journal of Advertising Research*—as well as an industry association—The Advertising Research Foundation—were established in 1936. Other journals followed and formal academic programs in marketing research were established at major universities throughout the United States.

During the late 1970s, it became increasingly apparent that public relations differed considerably from other communications disciplines, and advertising in particular, in its ability to be measured and evaluated. At the time, advertising testing was dominated by a variety of measurement and evaluation systems, of which the "day after recall" method (*DAR*), popularized by Burke Marketing Research in its work with Procter & Gamble, was one of the most common systems in use. These advertising-focused methods took on a source orientation and assumed that the message was completely controlled by the communicator.[8] Therefore the ability to test message recall and message efficacy were highly controllable and, in theory, projectable as to what would occur if the advertising were actually to be placed.

With the recognition that public relations needed a different set of measures because of the unique nature of the profession, senior management at several major public relations agencies charged their research departments with the task of finding more credible and reliable methods to measure the effectiveness of public relations activities. While a number of experiments were undertaken at that time, the primary benefit derived from this experimentation was a heightened awareness of the overall value of measuring public relations.

This heightened awareness, along with advances in specific technologies, led to the founding of a number of research companies during the 1980s and 1990s that specialize in measuring and evaluating the *outcome* of public relations activities as well as the founding of a trade association (International Association for Measurement and Evaluation of Communication formerly known as the Association of Media Evaluation Companies, AMEC www.amecorg.com),[9] the Commission on Public Relations Research and Evaluation and the Research Fellows both of which are affiliated with the Institute for Public Relations (www.instituteforpr. org).[10] Currently approximately two dozen companies offer services that measure and evaluate public relations activities.[11] These companies have traditionally focused on evaluating only the outcomes of public relations, most commonly as media or press coverage that is a direct result of media relations activities (*outputs*). Few of their staff have formal or academic research training outside of "on-the-job" training in content analysis, and unlike other forms of communications research, these companies typically place little emphasis on formative, programmatic, or diagnostic research or research that is used to develop communications strategies and evaluate the impact of communications activities on target audiences.

The primary limitation of these companies is their focus on an intermediary in the public relations process—the media—rather than on the target audiences for these communications activities.

While the legacy of these public relations research agencies, as well as the services they provide the public relations industry, is noteworthy, for the most part they have failed to significantly advance either the science or the art of public relations measurement and evaluation because of their strong emphasis on media relations.

This lack of advancement occurred despite an insistence and commitment by the leadership of the profession that research function as a key and essential element in the creation of effective and successful public relations programs. Industry leaders who demanded the use of research in the development and evaluation of public relations programs included luminaries such as Harold Burson (Burson-Marsteller), Daniel Edelman (Edelman Worldwide), and David Finn (Ruder Finn), each of whom established dedicated research functions in their respective agencies.

The most significant commitment of the industry leadership to this nascent discipline was the founding in 1956 of the Foundation for Public Relations Research and Education (now operating as the Institute for Public Relations [IPR]) in conjunction with the Public Relations Society of America (PRSA). Over the past 50 years, the foundation has continued to emphasize the critical importance of research in the public relations process and has dedicated itself to "the science beneath the art of public relations." Yet even with this dedicated effort, the IPR struggles to get the public relations profession and public relations professionals to recognize the importance of research and measurement as an essential element in the development of effective public relations programs. This struggle continues in spite of ongoing programs, conferences, and educational forums that focus exclusively on this agenda.

Moving Toward Excellence in Public Relations Research

While the IPR has been a continuing beacon on issues surrounding the inclusion of research in all public relations efforts, the shift toward using research to establish the foundation of public relations practice achieved its most significant support during the 1980s. In 1984, the International Association of Business Communicators (IABC) Foundation (now the IABC Research Foundation) developed a request for proposals for the landmark study of *Excellence in Public Relations and Communication Management*—a project that produced three books, many reports, and dozens of seminars for professionals on creating excellence in the practice of public relations.

In its request for proposals, the IABC board asked for proposals for research that would demonstrate how, why, and to what extent communication contributes to the achievement of organizational objectives and how the public relations function should be organized to best achieve those objectives. The foundation awarded a $400,000 grant to a team that included Professors James E. Grunig and Larissa Grunig of the University of Maryland and Professor David Dozier of San Diego State University.

This team, among others, produced numerous publications on excellence in public relations practice that include five major volumes.[12] *Excellence in Public Relations and Communication Management* by James Grunig; *Manager's Guide to Excellence in Public Relations and Communication Management* by David Dozier, Larissa Grunig and James Grunig;

Excellent Public Relations and Effective Organizations: A Study of Communication Management in Three Countries by James Grunig, Larissa Grunig and David Dozier; *Managing Public Relations* by James Grunig and Professor Todd Hunt; and *The Future of Excellence in Public Relations and Communication Management: Challenges for the Next Generation* by Professor Elizabeth Toth.

In addition, the Arthur W. Page Society underwrote one of the earliest and most business-oriented research volumes, *Using Research in Public Relations: Applications to Program Management* by Professor Glen Broom and David Dozier.[13]

Twenty-five years later, this remains the single largest grant in this field for the development of research protocols and practices. Yet even with this effort, the inclusion of research as a basic tool in the day-to-day practice of public relations remains an elusive goal.

During this period the profession has seen growth that is best represented by the multitude of companies specializing in this area, as well as a growing amount of academic literature in the field. Yet even with the increased attention paid, significant variations continue to exist in the range of approaches to public relations measurement and evaluation. These variations have resulted in a lack of standard measures that can be used to gauge the success of a public relations program, as well as in an uneven overall quality of the research being conducted.

There are likely many reasons why research in support of public relations activities has failed to progress significantly over the past 60 years. The reasons cited for this lack of advancement range from a genuine lack of commitment by the profession to a lack of resources, to a proprietary approach to research as a business edge, to changes in the practice of public relations, among others. However, there is another area where public relations research has failed and which is most likely the greatest contributor to its limited growth. That failure has been a systematic lack of understanding and application of the best practices necessary to achieve the levels of excellence required to advance the use of research to support the practice of public relations and, in turn, advance the overall practice of public relations.

The Concept of Best Practices

The history of "best practices" originated in the business literature during the origins of the industrial era.[14] The concept was that, while there are multiple approaches that can be used to achieve a task or a goal, there is often a single technique, method, or process that is more effective than others in reaching an established goal. In essence, a best practice is a technique, a method, a process, or an activity that is more effective at delivering a particular outcome than any other technique, method, process, or activity. By using best practices, projects, tasks, and activities can be accomplished more effectively and with fewer problems and complications.

There is an essential relationship between public relations research and practice. In particular, there is the relationship between evaluation and measurement and successful public relations practices. The focus of this book will be on what has been labeled "best practices in public relations measurement and evaluation systems."[15] Public relations best practices include (1) clear and well-defined research objectives, (2) rigorous research design, and (3) detailed supporting documentation. The quality and substance of the research findings (1) demonstrate effectiveness, (2) link outputs (tactics) to outcomes, (3) develop better communications programs, (4) demonstrate an impact on business outcomes, (5) demonstrate cost-effectiveness, and (6) are applicable to a broad range of activities.

As Figure 1.1 demonstrates, there is a strong interrelationship between the organization setting communication objectives, messages sent by the organization, how those messages are received, and how the outtakes from those messages impact on the objectives and goals set by the organization.

As noted in a commentary from PricewaterhouseCoopers, "Best practices are simply the best way to perform a business process. They are the means by which leading companies achieve top performance, and they serve as goals for other companies that are striving for excellence."[16]

While the concept of best practices is often applied to the operations of a specific company, the logical extension of best practices is its application to an overall industry through the establishment of standards against which assessments can be made. The goal of this book is to present best practices as they apply to public relations research, measurement, and evaluation. This presentation of best practices is not to provide definitive answers to business problems associated with communication. Rather, these best practices are meant

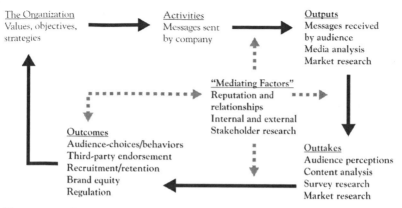

Figure 1.1. Best practices in public relations.
Used with permission of *Public Relations Journal*.

to be sources of creative insight for improving the application of public relations research and, in turn, for improving the overall quality and effectiveness of public relations activities.

What This Book Will Cover

Specifically, this book will provide business readers with a basic understanding of the problems and promises of public relations research, measurement, and evaluation, while providing public relations professionals, present and future, with a guide to the effective use of research methods and measures, and analytical insight that leads to meaningful evaluation in providing grounded evidence of the success (or failure) of public relations campaigns, as well as the necessary information to plan an effective campaign.[17]

A Practitioner's Guide to Public Relations Research, Measurement, and Evaluation is divided into five broad parts broken into short chapters:

- **Part I—Business and the Practice of Public Relations**

    This part covers three key areas that are essential to the creation of any effective public relations research. The first is a review of basic public relations theory and how public relations activities can be tied to predicting measureable business outcomes (chapter 1).

The second is a detailed examination of public relations goals and objectives in light of measureable business objectives. Included in this review is a discussion of what public relations goals and objectives can be realistically achieved and acceptable measures for each of these basic goals and objectives (chapter 2).

The third is a discussion of the elements of establishing achievable public relations goals in light of overall business objectives and then reviewing the processes for setting communications objectives that are active, measurable, and can be evaluated (chapter 3).

- **Part II—Qualitative Methods for Effective Public Relations Research, Measurement, and Evaluation**

  This part reviews the four major methodological areas that are commonly used in public relations research, measurement, and analysis. This part covers historical/secondary research (chapter 4); qualitative research, including in-depth interviews, focus groups, and participant observation and quantitative research (chapter 5); and content analysis (chapter 6). This part will also introduce the use of baseline and benchmark measurements and their effective application, historical research methods, and how to best use secondary research sources as part of a complete public relations research program. Particular emphasis will be placed on content analysis as one of the most commonly used and misused public relations methodologies, as well as on quantitative methods.

- **Part III—Quantitative Methods for Effective Public Relations Research, Measurement, and Evaluation**

  This part focuses on the quantitative dimension of public relations research, beginning with an emphasis on survey research (chapter 7). Descriptive statistics and the presentation of data (chapter 8) are examined as the baseline for understanding quantitative analysis as well as the concepts of probability and generalizing to larger audiences or populations. Finally, a discussion of sampling (chapter 9) rounds out the part.

- **Part IV—Best Practices of Public Relations Research, Measurement, and Evaluation**

    The final part of this book looks at the future of public relations research and the specific practices that will ensure the value of research in creating effective and valuable public relations programs (chapter 10).

Finally, the appendices include a bibliography of research and measurement sources, the *Dictionary of Public Relations Research and Measurement.*

Taken together, each of these parts will provide practitioners as well as nonpractitioners with a basic understanding of what is needed to evaluate public relations campaigns and ensure that research, measurement, and evaluation "toolkits" are up to date and complete.

CHAPTER 2

The Business of Public Relations

In chapter 1 we introduced the concept of best practices through the history of public relations research. In this chapter we will introduce and discuss the role of public relations as it relates to the larger goals and objectives of the organization. Public relations' impact on an organization's *return on investment* (ROI) is a fairly new concept. As the profession has turned from a tactical role to the strategic management of communications, the profession has had to continually wrestle with having to prove its worth. As part of the "promotional mix" of communications, public relations works in conjunction with advertising and marketing as an integral tool. Typically the promotional component (advertising, marketing, or public relations) most likely to meet an organization's communications needs and objectives takes the lead in creating programs and setting the communications agenda.[1] Up to the last decade, that lead almost always has fallen to marketing. Consequently, since the early 1990s, significant proportions of public relations activities, other than media relations, were expected to help support product marketing. Today, however, that role and the move toward truly integrated communications have put public relations—and corporate communications more specifically—at a different and more substantive level in organizations, as noted in the Arthur W. Page Society's seminal monograph *The Authentic Enterprise.*[2]

Establishing the Public Relations Campaign

Based on this discussion, it should be clear that a public relations approach to any business goal or objective necessarily incorporates research as a cornerstone in the development, refinement, and evaluation of that campaign. Boston University Professor Donald K. Wright has gone so far as to state that "if you don't have research on the front end and evaluation on the end, it isn't PR."[3] Wright stresses the role of research and theory in public relations. Wright states that there are four basic assumptions to public relations research in daily practice, assumptions that reflect a best practices approach to public relations research:[4]

1. The decision-making process is basically the same in all organizations [businesses].
2. All communication [programming and] research should
   - set objectives;
   - determine a strategy that establishes those objectives; and
   - implement tactics that bring those strategies to life.
3. All campaign research can be divided into three general phases:
   - development (initial research helping to establish goals and objectives);
   - refinement (continuous evaluation on expected benchmarks once the campaign is initiated and initiation of changes as deemed necessary to meet campaign goals and objectives);
   - evaluation (a final review of the campaign aimed at establishing its success or failure for not only the business, but also public relations goals and objectives).
4. Communication research is behavior-driven and knowledge [theory] based.

The final assumption drives home the challenge of public relations research as a mediating factor—that public relations programming and its measurement and evaluation strive to impact on stake- and stockholder behavior through the management of message-based programming that impacts on awareness, interest, attitudes, and intended behavior. Based on these assumptions, it should be clear that public relations that follows best practices first does the necessary background or competitive analyses that will help drive the public relations effort. It is during the developmental phase or stage that goals and objectives are created that support the business' goals and objectives.

Understanding Goals and Objectives

It is important to understand that goals and objectives are different in several important ways. A goal is a *projected* outcome that is desired.[5] Hence a goal might be to sell or lease *x* number of automobiles, reduce absenteeism, or to get more positive media attention for a product.

Goals are expectations and are fairly open as to results. An objective, on the other hand, is "an explicit statement [or statements] that support[s] a communication strategy."[6] In all too many cases, public relations campaigns suffer because they confuse goals with objectives, leading to inabilities to demonstrate impact or influence on business goals and objectives.

Public relations objectives are no different from marketing and advertising objectives in one critical sense—the need for establishing a campaign baseline and benchmarks needs to be stressed in every instance. Quite simply, without a starting point or baseline research results, public relations cannot demonstrate campaign success or failure. Further, without projected benchmarks it is difficult to demonstrate how strategy and tactics impact on campaign goals. Unfortunately, most public relations campaigns today fail to establish the beginning baseline and set expected benchmarks throughout the campaign. As related to Wright's assumptions, Figure 2.1 demonstrates the relationship between the baseline benchmark, planned benchmarks, and continuous testing of the

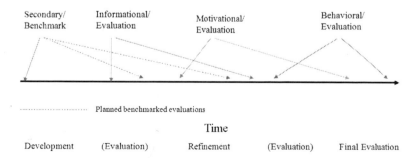

Figure 2.1. Planned benchmarking.
Used with permission of author and Guilford Press.

campaign.[7] Best practice campaign management would set multiple planned benchmarks to establish campaign effectiveness and allow for revision of objectives if necessary.

Stating the Objective

All research and evaluation planning should end with formal statements of the campaign's objectives. These objectives need to be related to overall business goals and objectives and can be more specific, relating to specific outcomes during the campaign. In general, the objective takes the form of a "to" statement: to do something that by such a date is expected to result in an outcome. Hence a business objective might be, "To gain a 10% market share by the end of third quarter sales through enhanced communications programs." The business goal would be to increase market share.

From a best practices approach, the objective should have been written with a benchmark for comparison or against the initial campaign baseline. Hence a better objective would have been "*To increase market share from 7% [baseline] to 10% by the end of third quarter sales through enhanced communication programs.*" The enhanced communication programs could then be further defined in terms of public relations, advertising, and marketing goals and objectives.

Public Relations Objectives

To better comprehend what public relations objectives are it is important to understand the three basic functions of public relations in any business campaign. According to Stacks,[8] all public relations activities fulfill three basic functions:

- First, the public relations function is to get necessary information out to the appropriate audience. An audience that behaves without understanding why it did so cannot be expected to do so again; hence an important function is to ensure that the information necessary for any intended action is available and has been understood—this is stated as an *informational objective*. This information can include general awareness of a product, service, or issue, as well as detailed knowledge.

- Second, once it has been established that the information has been (a) received and (b) understood, then the information's effect must be measured and evaluated—whether attitudes, beliefs, or values have been shaped, changed, or reinforced. This is stated as a *motivational objective*.

- Third, once it has been verified that the information has been received, understood, and has had an impact on the audience it must be determined whether the campaign has influenced the audience to take the *intended action*, such as a stated intent to purchase. This is stated as a *behavioral objective*.

The relationship between the three objective types should be clear. If the information is not reaching the target audiences, then the campaign's media relations strategy has not done what it was expected to do and research into the media channels employed must be reexamined. If the information has been received but not understood, then research must establish why—as Michaelson and Griffin did when they examined MetLife news stories and found systematic reporting problems confusing the target audience—and corrective action taken to put the campaign back on track.[9] (This study will be examined in more detail in chapter 6; it is the first study to measure reporting errors by the media and suggest remedial action to reduce them.) Once the information has been received and understood, then the audience must be evaluated to establish effect or impact. If the campaign is to change attitudes toward a product, is it actually doing so? If so, has that change been what was planned? If not, the message strategy must be reexamined. The informational and motivational objectives lead to the final public relations objective— the campaign outcome is such that the audience intends to behave as expected—and the public relations campaign has contributed to business objectives and goals.

Stating Public Relations Research Objectives

From a measurement and evaluation point of view, most public relations objectives fall woefully short of being precise enough to establish what kinds of research methods are required. Obviously the type of research being conducted will differ in terms of cost. In-depth interviews are more expensive than surveys, for instance, in terms of understanding how audiences will or have responded to a campaign. Also, the measurement and evaluation of the campaign is influenced by the public relations tactics being employed. Future chapters will explore the various methods public relations researchers employ to measure outcomes. In this section we examine the research subobjectives associated with public relations objectives.

For each public relations objective there should be at least one research objective. These research objectives determine which research methods should be employed, when they should be employed, and the expected outcome.[10] If the informational objective is "to increase auto purchasers knowledge of the 2010 models from 2009 [baseline] through increased use of employee blogging [tactic] by 9% [informational outcome]," the research objective should state how and when measurement and evaluation is to take place. Thus a public relations research objective might be

> *To gather data from social media users [audience] who intend to purchase a new auto on their understanding of new models [continuing informational outcome] to ascertain if intended purchasing has increased from benchmark [behavioral outcome]. The most appropriate way to collect these data is through an Internet-based web survey [method] three times during the first and second quarters of 2010 [time frame].*

Other methods employed might include conducting focus groups of audience members, content analyses of reactions to employee blogs, tracking website requests for more information, and so forth. What the research objective does is to specify methods.

Public Relations Role as Defined
at the Managerial Level

Public relations historically has focused primarily on media relations—getting the message out. It was not until the last 20 years or so that the focus of public relations has shifted to the strategic value it provides on the organization's ROI. This change from a strictly media-relations perspective to one that includes a broader strategic management perspective can be seen in how public relations' *outputs*—communications materials that are produced to support the corporation—have changed over the years.[11] Figure 2.2 shows the early relationships between marketing, advertising, and public relations. Here we can see that in traditional practice, marketing drives advertising, which in turn drives public relations.

Influence, starting with marketing, originates at the far left. Why? Because marketing provides hard data on what it drives toward the investment put into it; advertising provides numeric data based on circulation figures that reflect awareness, interest, and intent to purchase—data that may be of questionable use, but backed by considerable secondary data on *potential* purchasers of a product or service.[12] On the other hand, public relations provides little numeric data beyond the number of press materials sent out and the number of articles that contain information from those press materials.

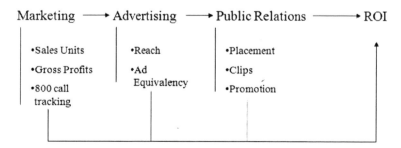

Figure 2.2. Traditional perspectives on the relationships between marketing, advertising, and PR.
Used with permission of author and Guilford Press.

When using a strategic management approach, however, contemporary public relations assumes a different role, one that divides promotional communications (e.g., marketing, advertising, and public relations) *outcomes* into two classes of *indicators*: financial and nonfinancial (see Figure 2.3).

Understanding Nonfinancial Indicators

Since nonfinancial indicators are not "hard," how are they measured? Basically all nonfinancial indicators are subjective and exist in the minds of the public or target audience a client seeks to influence. To demonstrate impact, a nonfinancial indicator—often referred to as "key performance indicators"—must show how it relates to a business goal or objective. That is, in the mixed-marketing model, for example, how does the public relations effort impact on awareness, knowledge, interest, and intent to purchase? In an employee relations effort, how does managerial relationship affect employee morale or absenteeism?

The nonfinancial indicators that have demonstrated public relations "value" and impact are perceptual. They are social and psychological in nature and, as such, must be approached using subjective, yet reliable and

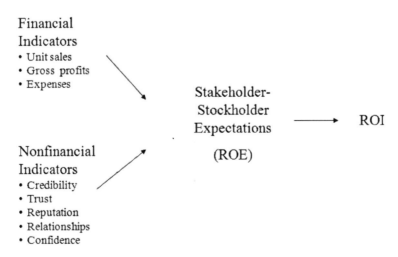

Figure 2.3. Contemporary thought on the relationships between marketing, advertising, and PR.
Used with permission of author and Guilford Press.

valid measurement. Yet even though they are perceptual, they clearly indicate an impact on the financial indicators and need to be treated in much the same way. Thus a public relations objective should find a way to demonstrate how the output is communicated to those who may influence the intended public or target audience to do something. This is done through specification of an *outtake*, a specified evaluation of a product, company, or idea by an opinion leader.[13] As noted earlier, an opinion leader—a stock analyst, political analyst, politician, or editorial endorsement—can change a target audience's perceptions of whatever it is that the opinion leader opines on. As noted in Figure 2.4, the variables the public relations professional can use via some messaging strategy have demonstrated influence on opinion leaders. Indeed, the public relations goal may be to improve client reputation through influencing—persuading—opinion leader reporting on that client.

Financial indicators traditionally include marketing and advertising outcomes, while public relations nonfinancial indicators deal with outcomes—defined as the "quantifiable changes in the awareness, knowledge, attitude, opinion, and behavior levels that occur as a result of a public relations program or campaign"—that can be demonstrated to impact an organization's social and financial goals and objectives.[14] While financial indicators deal with hard-core data, nonfinancial indicators deal with social data—perceptions, attitudes, and beliefs—that have

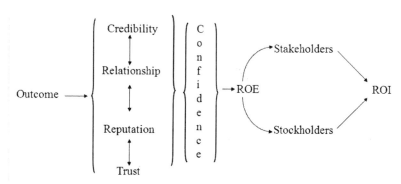

Figure 2.4. A strategic communication management model of PR influence on ROI.
Used with permission of author and Guilford Press.

demonstrated impact on what public relations refers to as "third-party endorsers."[15] Figure 2.2 also noted that the outcomes of interest from a promotional approach are mediated by the expectations of stake- or stockholders, but from the public relations perspective those expectations can be manipulated via carefully selected messages aimed at influential audience members (e.g., editors, analysts, or any opinion leaders).

These relationships for the nonfinancial indicators have been further conceptualized by Stacks as a working model of the relationships between and within the nonfinancial variables as demonstrated in Figure 2.3.[16] This represents a strategic model of communication management that can be parsed out to establish how much each variable contributes to the final ROI. As Stacks notes, these indicators can be written as a mathematical formula:

$$\text{Outcome} = \beta \pm [\text{Credibility} \pm \text{Relationship} \pm \text{Reputation} \pm \text{Trust}] \pm \text{Confidence} + \text{Error}.$$

In this formula, β is the starting point (in a promotional campaign) that is in turn influenced by credibility, relationship, reputation, and trust, and this is further modified by audience confidence. That confidence can be in the product, service, or even the overall organization and has an overall tolerance that can be described as error. This model allows the professional to classify specific outcomes as functions of the nonfinancial indicators that can be used to *predict* outcomes and provide guidance in communications decisions (see chapter 9, "Statistical Analysis").

Understand the Relationship to Financial Indicators

This model is not independent of the financial indicators, but works in conjunction with them, especially when public relations is approached from a mixed-marketing model.[17] In the mixed-marketing model, public relations efforts are focused on providing data that correlate directly to sales and have taken the form of approximated advertising indicators. These indicators—advertising value equivalency, reach, and circulation, for instance—try to establish the value of *placed* public relations activities when compared to the actual paid value of an advertisement. The problem with such indicators is that they do not reflect value, but reflect costs associated with placement. While advertisers can specify where their material is placed in the various media (the more prominent, the greater the cost), public relations placements cannot be guaranteed. In fact, the Commission on Public Relations Measurement and Evaluation no longer accepts pseudo-advertising as representing true public relations value, while attempting to identify better measures of impact on ROI.

The Challenge of Establishing Public Relations Effect on ROI

The challenge for public relations is to establish a relationship between financial indicators and the nonfinancial indicators that also influence a business' "bottom line," which is now more than simply financial and has added social responsibility and ecology (e.g., the "triple bottom line"). For instance, how does a company's relationship with its customers impact on sales performance? How does reputation impact on stock prices? What happens when a trusted company does something "bad"? Are "green" companies more socially responsible and profitable? A recent Edelman "Goodpurpose" study reported by *PR Week* "found that 61% of consumers worldwide have purchased a brand that supports a good cause even if it wasn't the cheapest brand," which demonstrates the impact of social responsibility as a public relations outcome.[18]

The correlation between a financial indicator and a nonfinancial indicator is the first step. A second step is to show, over time, how the nonfinancial indicators influence company outcome. We know, for instance, that it only takes one bad analyst report on a publically traded company to drop stock prices. Further, we know that consumer confidence in a company can drive sales, stock prices, and other business outcomes. Third, we need to look at these relationships based on how they have influenced business goals and objectives from a set point in time—a benchmark against which comparisons and strategic decisions can be made.

Finally, the public relations effort should be viewed in terms of the traditional outcome model associated with promotional communication. That is, each phase of the public relations campaign must clearly understand what part of the campaign it is being employed in and the campaign's strategy associated with it. For instance, is the campaign to introduce a new brand? In that case, its goal is most likely to establish awareness of the brand. If awareness is not a goal, then perhaps it is increasing interest and understanding of the brand. If awareness and interest and understanding are present, then perhaps the campaign is to create a desire for the brand. If awareness, interest, understanding, and desire are present, then perhaps the campaign's goal is to influence adoption of the brand.

These goals can be stated more precisely by looking at what nonfinancial variables are most relevant for the brand over a campaign. Attitudinal outcomes such as increased homophily or authority might be part of the campaign's strategy in a new brand introduction,[19] or reputation variables such as social responsibility and company familiarity[20] might be used to influence intentions to purchase. In the end, however, the public relations outcomes must have a demonstrated correlation to business outcome; that is, ROE must demonstrate impact on ROI.

Summary

This chapter introduced the reader to the relationships between public relations and business goals and objectives. The public relations effort does not exist in a vacuum, but works closely with business goals and objectives, whether they are financial or nonfinancial. By now readers should have a basic understanding of outputs, outtakes, and outcomes and how they relate to the public relations effort. Further, the reader should understand the importance of setting realistic and measurable objectives.

Part II examines the major research methods employed by public relations to gather the information (data) necessary to evaluate the public relations effort. Part II begins with the gathering of existing information through historical and secondary data. It then examines the use of content analysis—perhaps the most common of the methods used by public relations researchers. Following content analysis, qualitative methods are explored—in-depth interviews, focus groups, and participant observation. The last two chapters focus on the quantitative gathering of data through an understanding of sampling, survey, and polling methodologies.

CHAPTER 3

Measuring Public Relations Outcomes

Previous chapters alluded to the need for public relations professionals to understand and measure the outcomes they hope to achieve in their campaign programming. This is not a new topic, yet it increased in importance in the last decade of the 20th century as the profession sought to be able to demonstrate effectiveness. Public relations measurement, as noted in chapter 2, often deals with what academics call "mediating" or "intermediary" variables—things that impact on the final business outcome but are not necessarily financial in nature. Organizational, brand, and product credibility are examples; something that cannot be "seen" but can be measured and verified as a valid and reliable *predictor* of final outcome. This chapter introduces the reader to measurement and evaluation from a social scientific perspective, one that allows the public relations professional to create reliable and valid measures of nonfinancial indicators (see chapter 2). The chapter will differentiate between "hard" financial indicators and "soft" nonfinancial indicators. As discussed previously, nonfinancial indicators include, but are not limited to, measures of confidence, credibility, relationship, reputation, trust, and indicators of awareness, interest and understanding, desire, and intent to adopt.[1]

Fundamentals of Data and Measurement

What does it mean when someone says that they are measuring something? Does it mean that what is being measured is observable? Does it establish differences or similarities between objects of measurement? Is it something that comes naturally? Is it done to create data that can be used to establish relationships between things? Finally, does it "mean" anything in particular? All of these are questions that measurement researchers ask daily when they try to create, use, and evaluate measures for any use. Public relations measurement researchers are no different, except that they have entered the process a little later than their promotional communication colleagues.

So what does it mean when we say we are measuring something? It means that we are establishing a ruler that allows for comparison and interpretation of the "data" obtained from those measures.[2] For instance, in the physical world, measurement is fairly straightforward; we often use inches, centimeters, yards, meters, miles, and so forth to measure linear distance (although it is unclear from this whether we are talking about horizontal or vertical distance). What we have established, however, is a *metric* that can be used to describe something—distance or height in this case. However, in the social world we also measure things that are not as observable, but are "potentially observable"—credibility, reputation, and trust, to name but a few things. Based on our created nonfinancial measures, we can then make decisions as to whether something is longer or shorter, higher in credibility, or lower in trust when compared against something else.

Notice, however, that the interpretation of the measurement is usually less precise than the measure itself. Measurement interpretation often says something is heavier than something else—and in many instances this can be done with different measures, "pounds" of personal weight as compared to "stones" of personal weight. While measurement is more precise and can be tested for its reliability and validity, interpretation is determined with words.

Measurement as a Public Relations Tool

At its simplest, measurement is an observation. From a business perspective, measurement is used to track financially related variables. These variables include the number of units produced, stock prices, gross and net profits, and so forth. Their measurement is quite precise because the data are "hard"; that is, they are directly observable and can be "counted." Marketing can tell how many products are sold per 1-800-phone call-in and can calculate the cost per call across a number of other hard data points—number of hours staff put in, returns, and so forth (see chapter 2). Human resources can provide a breakdown of cost per unit by employee and employee costs (wages and benefits, for instance).

From a public relations perspective, measurement is less precise because the data are "soft." Soft data are not easily observed, which is one reason why investment in public relations measurement has suffered. Instead of focusing on the mediating variables that affect business outcome, public relations *counted* simple indicators of distribution. As such, the "clip book" measures success in the number of releases sent out and picked up in the media (numbers), the story's placement in the media (could be measured as above or below the fold, page number, presence or absence of an accompanying photograph), or as the equivalent cost of comparable advertising (a measure that the Commission on Public Relations Measurement and Evaluation has deemed inappropriate and misleading, but many use).[3] Since the mid-1990s, measurement has become important to public relations because public relations theory, driven hard by public relations academics and some professionals who have backgrounds in anthropology, communication, psychology, and sociology, has argued hard for the mediating impact of public relations and demanded that public relations measurement begin to focus on nonfinancial variables on bottom-line results. This is not to say that simple counts are invalid; they are just one of a number of measurement tools the professional can use to demonstrate effectiveness, but they are not as precise, nor do they provide the data required to demonstrate impact on the bottom line.

Once it is established that reliable and valid nonfinancial measures can be created, their effectiveness during and after the campaign as related to financial indicators can be assessed. This provides the public relations professional with a way to actually establish campaign impact against planned benchmarks, compare public relations effectiveness as related to ancillary marketing and advertising indicators, and at campaign's end, demonstrate impact on final return on investment (ROI) within the public relations department and the general business as a whole.

So what exactly should public relations measurement be concerned with? Where there are hard data based on financially related measures, it should be gathered, interpreted, and evaluated. Where there are soft data based on nonfinancially related measures, those measures should be created or, if available from academic or business sources, adapted, gathered, interpreted, and evaluated. In the end, both sets of data—financial and nonfinancial—should be used to assess the impact on public relations and general business goals and objectives. Nonfinancial measures are related to particular publics' or audiences' values, beliefs, and attitudes—variables that, from the social sciences, we know impact on decision making.[4]

Data and Measurement

Measurement is *a systematic process of observing and recording observations as data.*[5] Data *are the observations themselves* that are used for comparative or descriptive purposes. As noted earlier, financial and nonfinancial data are different in that financial data can actually be counted, while nonfinancial data must be collected as reflecting an individual's values, beliefs, and attitudes. The collection of data differs then in that nonfinancial data come from measurements developed to assess an individual's opinions that reflect their inner thinking processes. This is covered later; for now, the basics of data need to be addressed.

Basically data can be defined as existing in four distinctly different forms or levels. Further, these levels are systematically linked by how they are defined. How the particular data are defined influences how they are interpreted and ultimately evaluated. The definitional process begins by establishing whether the data are based on categories (*categorical data*) or along a continuum (*continuous data*). Further, in terms of evaluation, data that are defined as continuous are generally more powerful (they provide more information about the observations in terms of being able to calculate the mean, standard deviation, and variance of observations) than data that are categorical, which can only be reported as simple counts, percentages, or simple proportions. Hence we have two types of data that can each be subdivided into two levels.

Categorical Data

At the categorical level we have *nominal data*, data that is defined simply by systematically naming the observations but making no assessment beyond the names. For instance, there are many different ways that public relations is practiced. Distinguishing between corporate and agency, for instance, is a measurement of public relations practice that simply distinguishes between two of many different practice units. The measure says nothing about which is more important, which is more effective, which is more representative, or which has more professionals practicing in the area. Traditional public relations measurement dealing with the number of press releases "picked up" by the media would produce nominal data; the measure tells us how many releases were picked up in various papers, but not the quality of the release or whether the stories were accurate.

As noted earlier, the role of nominal measurement is to simply differentiate between subcategories of some outcome variable. For instance, a public relations campaign may want to get a simple indication of an attributed message source's credibility or of several potential attributed sources. The simplest and probably most direct measure would be to ask people whether they thought the sources were credible: "In your opinion is so-and-so a believable source? Yes or No." Similarly, one of the authors, in conducting public relations for gubernatorial candidates in the late 1970s, asked survey respondents, "Who is the governor of Alabama?" and then checked off the names reported. Each name was equal to other names; hence the measurement was nominal. Finally, intent to purchase or recommend purchase is often measured via a simple "Do you intend to purchase/recommend stock in company X? Yes or No."

If we define our measurement system as more than simply distinguishing by assessing some relative quality—large or small, expensive or cheap, tall or short—then the measurement system produces *ordinal data*, data that order the observations systematically based on some criteria clearly defined in advance. Thus we could measure public relations units by the number of clients they have, by their net income, or by the number of employees they have (large, medium, small). The measurement creates an ordered set of data that differs on some preassigned quality. Of importance to ordinal data is that there be no overlap between categories. For instance, age is a variable that is difficult to get survey responses to when respondents are asked, "What is your age in years?" People often refuse to answer or will "stretch" their responses from the truth. The same is true of income questions. Ordinal measurement provides a way around both problems by establishing a systematic system: age may be under 18, 19–25, 26–50, 51–65, or over 65 and income may be under $10,000, $11,000–$20,000, $21,000–$50,000, or over $50,000. Note that the categories are not equal, nor are they intended to be. Instead, they represent an ordered number of categories that meet some measurement criteria (could be based on previous research or could be from an analysis of U.S. Census data).

Ordinal measurement is often called "forced choice" measurement because respondents must choose a category or be placed in a nonresponsive category by the researcher. Hence an ordinal measure of credibility would take the form of naming a source and asking a respondent whether she was "very believable," "believable," or "not believable." Should the respondent not make a decision, he is placed in a "refused to answer" (RTA) category. An ordinal measure of awareness might be phrased, "How aware are you of the current governor of Alabama? Very Aware, Aware, Not Aware." For the intent to purchase measure, an ordinal measure might be stated as, "Company X is offering stock at $xx.xx, how sure are you about purchasing this stock? Will Definitely Purchase, May Purchase, May Not Purchase, Definitely Will Not Purchase." For both examples, refusal to answer for whatever reason results in the respondent being placed in the RTA category.

Continuous Data

Continuous data are found on a continuum and how that continuum is defined dictates what type of data they are. Continuous data that exist within an interval on the continuum are called *interval data* because it does not matter where the observation is within the interval, it is measured as being in that interval. It does not matter where in the interval the observation is, just that it is observed in that interval. Hence the difference between the numbers 1, 2, and 3 are exactly 1 unit from each (1 is one unit from 2 and two units from 1; 3 is two units from 1 and is one unit from 2). This will become more important a little later, but for now think of age as the variable being measured. Upon a birthday you are 1 year older, even though you may only be 1 day older than you were the day before. A majority of public relations measures produce interval data.[6]

The use of interval measures by public relations, as will be expanded on shortly, has been limited, primarily because the profession has employed a marketing approach to measurement that forces respondents to make a definite choice regarding the measurement object. Interval measurement requires that the perceived distance between points on the continuum appear to be equal, hence the forced choice does not allow a respondent to be "unsure," "uncertain," or "undecided." An interval measure would add an arbitrary midpoint among the categories, allowing respondents to be uncertain, and would make RTA a truly nonresponsive choice. Hence our interval measures for the earlier examples would allow for uncertainty. For our credibility measure, the responses would be "very believable," "believable," "neither believable nor not believable," "not believable," "very not believable." In the same manner, awareness responses would be "very aware," "aware," "neither aware nor unaware," "unaware," "not aware," and the intent responses would be "will definitely purchase," "may purchase," "may or may not purchase," "may not purchase," "definitely will not purchase."

Measures that produce data that can be found anywhere on a continuum that has a true zero point are called *ratio data*. Most hard financial data are interval in nature: units produced, employee work hours, gross or net income in dollars and cents. Further, since there is a true zero point (interval data may have a zero point, but it is arbitrary as to where it exists along a continuum), the measure can further be defined in terms of absolute difference from zero, hence it can be used to measure profit and loss.

Ratio measures are used in public relations even less than interval measures. A ratio measure asks respondents to make a decision based on where on a continuum they would fall regarding the object of measure. For instance, we might ask, "On a scale of 0 to 100, where 0 is the complete absence of credibility and 100 is completely credible, where would you place X?" The same would be done for awareness and intent.

Continuous data are found in nonfinancial measures, but primarily at the interval level. Public relations has not required the precision of ratio measures for a number of reasons, but primarily because the measurement of psychological indicators, of which credibility, relationship, reputation, and trust are commonly used measures, does not require that much precision. They measure what a person thinks; however, such measures have been correlated to actual behavior—what is expressed (opinion) and what is done. Ratio measures are also more difficult to administer and require sophisticated statistical knowledge to interpret and evaluate. Further, as evidenced by the thermometer example, which many would consider to be a ratio measure, the zero point (where water freezes) is arbitrary—either 0° Celsius or 32° Fahrenheit. The actual ratio measure would be in Kelvin, where 0K is equal to –237.59° C or –459.67° F. Such precision is not required in most public relations measurement systems.

Creating and Using Measurement Systems

To better understand measurement and evaluation, let us try something. In the left margin of page 33, put the total number of words contained on the page as a ratio measure. (Why is it a ratio? Because it can range from zero—no words—to the actual count you get.) Now count the number of sentences on the page and put that in the left margin as an interval measure. (Why interval? Because a single word can be a sentence if it has punctuation.) Now count the number of long, medium, and short sentences as an ordinal measure and put it in the left margin. (Why ordinal? Because you will have to come up with a rationale for what constitutes a long, a medium, and a short sentence—say long would be more than 10 words; medium between 9 and 4 words; short less than 4 words). Finally, count the number of nouns and then pronouns on the page and put them in the left margin.

Please turn back to page 33 and reread that page and then come back to this page. Now run your counts again and put what you observe in the right margin for each measurement level. Did you get the same results? If so, your counting is reliable and probably valid. If you did not get the *same* results (similar does not count), then you have just met two of measurement's problems: reliability and validity. We will return to both in a while, but for now think back on what you did the second time that might have created what we will call measurement "error."

Basically all measurement has some error in it. The job of good measurement is to keep that error as small as possible. This is done in several ways, from diligently creating a measurement system that can be employed by different people at different times producing the same results each time and by each person carefully looking at how that system is described or "operationalized."

Measuring Public Relations Outcomes

Based on what has been discussed thus far, it should be clear that public relations outcomes that have a direct impact on business goals and objectives are nonfinancial in nature. What this means is that public relations serves as a mediating or influencing factor on the final outcome of any campaign and its programming (outputs aimed at specific opinion leaders who will then serve as "third-party endorsers" of the campaign's message). These mediating factors are not readily apparent, but they are potentially observable. What this means is that public relations measures focus on the perceptions that publics and target audiences have of a business, company, brand, individual member, or whatever.

The problem with mediating variables is that they cannot be *directly* measured. Unlike financial-like data such as profits and losses, employee hours, or number of products produced, public relations variables exist in the *minds* of those individuals at whom the public relations effort is being targeted. Thus public relations measurement seeks to understand *perceptions* of the measurement object's qualities—perceptions of product or company credibility, reputation, trust, and the perceived relationship and confidence in that relationship those individuals have with the object of measurement.

So how does a public relations researcher measure something that cannot be seen? The answer is to do it as any social scientist would. Since the early 1900s, social scientists have measured with varying degrees of reliability and validity internal thoughts or perceptions.[7] What we know from this body of research is that behaviors can be inferred from people's expressions about something. That is, we know that behaviors are influenced by attitudes, beliefs, and values. The problem is that all reside in our mind, and although we can observe brain functioning through different forms of activity, we obviously do not have a way to peer into the deep recesses of the mind where attitudes, beliefs, and values "reside." What social scientists do is to correlate actual behavior with intended behavior—actual behavior being the action taken by an individual and intended behavior being the expressed course of action an individual *says* he will take. What an individual says he will do is defined as his *opinion* on some future or past action. We know from anthropological, communication, psychological, and sociological studies that opinions are the expression of *attitudes*, which are defined as predispositions to act in some way. Attitudes, in turn, are based on *belief systems*, which are more primitive and allow for fairly simple internal processing. Beliefs are formed based on value systems, which are so basic that most people do not actually think about them.[8]

Thus public relations researchers focus on creating measures that reflect the inner feelings and thoughts of their publics or targeted audiences. Creating such measures requires an understanding of culture and language: culture, because our culture tends to create our value systems; language, because people express their cognitive and affective responses to something through their language. Further, if measured carefully—which means that the measures are (a) measuring what we think they are measuring (are valid) and (b) do so time and again (are reliable)—they have been demonstrated to reflect actual behavior up to 60% of the time,[9] which is higher than would be expected from chance alone.

So public relations researchers assess outcomes based on systems of measurement that predict behavior. The problem comes in determining whether those measures are valid and reliable. With financial indicators— much like word counts on a page—the researcher can count and recount until she's certain that the number is correct. This is not possible with social and nonfinancial measures, as there are a multitude of things that may be operating at different times while measuring them. Add to this the real problem of businesses creating and then not sharing measures due to the "proprietary" nature of business in general, and it becomes clear that there are many nonfinancial measures and that their creation and validation may not be open to all (hence public relations researchers often have to rely on academics to create basic instruments and then adapt them to specific problems).

The problem, then, is creating reliable and valid measures of variables that will mediate the intended and actual behaviors of a public or target audience. Social scientists do this by creating attitudinal or belief *scales*, measures that collect data by asking questions or making statements that respondents answer or react to. Notice that the plural form is used here—questions and statements. When someone responds to a single statement or answers a single question (an "item") the researcher cannot be certain that the response is reliable. If reliability cannot be judged, validity cannot be established.

Measuring and Validating Nonfinancial and Social Variables

There are many measures found in the social sciences literature that can be adapted to public relations. However, unlike academic research, which can take months if not years to conduct, public relations professionals are rarely allowed much time to prepare and substantiate their measurement efforts. The rise of public relations research and measurement firms—some stand-alone and some as part of larger, multifunctional public relations agencies—has provided some movement toward measurement, but with the proprietary nature of the measurement efforts, these are not often shared with other professionals. Reports are written and presented of findings employing these measures, but the actual measures and how they are computed, weighted, and assessed rarely find their way into print. Therefore it is incumbent on the public relations professional to understand the basics of measuring social and nonfinancial variables. An informed client, after all, is the best client, and being able to participate in establishing a measurement system—even if done so quickly to collect data on ongoing programs—should provide a better and more targeted measure.

Creating Nonfinancial and Social Measures

As far back as the early 19th century, social scientists were creating measures of human behavior and measures that predict those behaviors. The earliest of those measures assessed attitudes, beliefs, and values. They did so through the use of language—that is, they understood that measures are dependent on the language people use to communicate and that not all languages have common meanings or phrases that are similar to other languages. These measures are called *measurement scales* and are composed of *items*—statements or bipolar wording groups—that when added and averaged provide the outcome measure of interest. Since public relations measurement is often done through polls and surveys or through carefully constructed questionnaires, only three of the many approaches to attitude measurement are actually used.

Equal Appearing Interval Scale. The oldest measurement system was developed by Thurstone and Chave in 1929.[10] In this system, an attitude or belief object was measured by what they called "equal appearing intervals." The intervals were actually numeric values of statements created and tested to range from one end of the attitudinal continuum to the other. Hence items were created and tested on a large sample of people from the population to be measured. Hundreds of statements about the attitude object were created and participants were asked to put each into one of 11 piles (from very unfavorable to very favorable, for instance) and then the statement's average was computed and its range of assigned favorableness was examined. From this analysis of hundreds of statements, a large number were determined to be valid and reliable items in a larger scale. Fifty to sixty of the items could then be given to participants who then indicated which they *agreed* with. The items agreed with were then summed and divided by the total number to create a score.

The advantage to Thurstone and Chave's measure is that it has validity for a large number of people based on preestablished values. Postadministration reliability should be high because of all the work done to prepare the scale items. The disadvantage comes from the amount of time it takes to create and validate the measure—something even more daunting in today's social networking media.

Likert-Type Measures. In 1932 Rensis Likert reported on a different attitude measure that has become a staple of public relations measurement.[11] Likert's system employed an odd-numbered response set to a simple statement to which respondents selected which response category best represented their feelings on the attitude object. Likert argued that with multiple statements focusing on the same attitude object, an "equal appearing interval" measure could be created that was reliable and valid. Where Likert differed from Thurstone and Chave was in the creation of a midpoint between positive and negative responses. Further, he stressed the need for each category to be a direct opposite of its linguistic partner. For instance, in the classic Likert-type scale, the opposites of "strongly agree" and "agree" are "disagree" and "strongly disagree." The midpoint is "neither agree nor disagree." However, the categories could just as easily be "excellent" and "good," which would be opposed by "bad" and "terrible." The problem comes with calling the attitude object "terrible"—something that most clients would prefer not knowing.

To become truly interval data, however, Likert argued that there must be multiple statements, at least two or three, and that they should be stated as degrees of opposition. For instance, the statement "I love brand X" would be opposed by "I hate brand X" and a middle-ground statement would be "I like brand X." These would then be randomly placed with other items and presented to a respondent in a paper-and-pencil measure. If the respondent agreed with the first statement, she should disagree with the second and be somewhere in the middle on the third statement. This provides a sort of internal reliability that can be observed through the paper-and-pencil markings.

Likert-type measures have the advantage that they can be created quite quickly and have demonstrated consistent reliability if created systematically following the validation steps discussed earlier. There are problems with languages other than English in terms of direct translation; the traditional "strongly agree" to "strongly disagree" category system does not work in Spanish or in Semitic languages such as Hebrew.

Semantic Differential Measures. In 1957 Charles Osgood, George Suci, and Percy Tannenbaum produced a different measurement system that relied not on categories but on a true continuum as bounded by bipolar words or phrases, which they labeled the "semantic differential."[12] Their work built on that of Thurstone and Chave and Likert and was a carefully conducted measurement program that identified a number of bipolar adjectives that were demonstrated to be valid and reliable measures of attitude. In particular, they found that a series of items could measure an attitude's cognitive, affective, and activity (behavioral) dimensions. The format of the measure, however, has limited its use. The measure consists of lines of items whose bipolar terms have been randomly reversed to require that each be carefully read. For instance, one of the dimensions regularly included in the activity dimension uses three items: active–passive, sharp–dull, and fast–slow. Each is separated by an odd number of spaces on the continuum between them and the respondent reads each and places a mark on the continuum where her perception of an attitude object belongs:

Brand X

Active	____:____:____:____:____:____:____	Passive
Sharp	____:____:____:____:____:____:____	Dull
Slow	____:____:____:____:____:____:____	Fast

When used with paper-and-pencil responses, the semantic differential is a reliable measure of any attitude, object, or even a position stated as a sentence (e.g., "Health care should be universal for all Americans"). It is important that the visual nature of the measure be maintained, a problem with many web-based survey programs, and it is almost impossible to use in a person-to-person interview or telephone survey.

Establishing Scale Reliability and Validity

As noted earlier in this chapter, measurement reliability and validity are major concerns when constructing a measurement system or instrument. Reliability means that what you are measuring will be measured the same way each time. Validity means that you are actually measuring what you say you are measuring. Interestingly, to establish validity, you must first establish reliability—a measure that is not reliable is never valid.[13]

Reliability. An alarm set for 7:00 a.m., if reliable, should go off at 7:00 each morning. But the question then becomes, is it actually a valid measure of time? If the clock is set 5 minutes fast, when the alarm goes off, is it actually 6:55? Further, are you certain after only one "test" that the alarm will go off on time later? We first looked at this a few pages ago when we talked about the problem with one-item measures. A response to a single "test" can never establish reliability—the behavior (marking as with a pencil or physically observing a behavior) could be random or could be a clear observation of what happened; *the problem is we do not know, and what we do not know we cannot explain.* Hence we need repeated observations stated in different ways to ascertain a measure's reliability.

We also know that unlike the hard sciences or in measures that do not involve humans (such as learning psychology's white mice studies), humans, due to the nature of their ability to construct abstraction, rarely are 100% reliable over time. Thus what measurement attempts to do is to establish what is called a reliability index that ranges from 0.00 (completely unreliable) to 1.00 (completely reliable). This index is expressed in what we know about (systematic error or known variance among measurement participants) and what we do not know (random error or unknown variance among measurement participants) stated as systematic error divided by random error. Further, if we take the reliability finding, square it, and then subtract it from 1.00, we have an index of what we do not know about measurement reliability. Thus if a measure is reported to have a reliability of 0.90, we find that 81% of the variance in responding to the measure is known or systematic error ("good" error—we can explain it) and 19% of the variance is still random error ("bad" error—we cannot explain it). So even a measure that is 90% reliable is almost 20% unreliable. A figure of 95% is a commonly used standard in public relations research. However, Stacks suggests that 90% or better reliability is excellent, 80%–90% reliability is good, and anything less than 80% requires that the measure be approached with caution.[14]

Validity. Validity—whether we are measuring what we think we are measuring—is more than a philosophical concern. If we think we are measuring reputation, but instead are measuring something else, then all the results—the "hard" data obtained from which to correlate other, financial indicators—will be worthless. In academia, where time and "subjects" (students who typically gain course credit for participating in a measure's creation and validation) are plentiful, a measure is created in four basic steps: steps 1 and 2 address validity, step 3 addresses reliability, and step 4 provides indicators of actual usefulness.

The first step in any measurement system is to do the necessary secondary research to understand exactly what is to be measured. This "due diligence" step produces *face validity*, or validity based on the measurement researcher's knowledge of the subject and other extant measures. The measure at this stage is only as valid as the amount of research time put into secondary research (to include studying about measurement—*psychometrics*) and the researcher's own credibility. Once the researcher has completed a large set of *potential* items, she turns to the second stage for what is called content validity. Step 2 requires that others who are knowledgeable in the subject examine each item to ensure that the items do indeed relate to what the researcher thinks she is going to measure. Further, because individual researchers often do not see where conflicts or contradictions may occur, this panel of "experts" can point out where items are poorly stated—they may not relate to the attitude object or they may be *double-barreled*, having two or more possible meanings so that responses to the item are never fully understood; they usually are words or phrases joined by "and," "but," or "or." Once the researcher has examined the item pool and the evaluation of the expert panel, she may move on to step 3.

Step 3 examines the measure for its construct validity. *Construct validity* deals with how respondents actually see the entire measurement scale. People evaluate attitude objects in three dimensions: what they think of them (*cognitive*); how they react to them (*affective*); and how they plan on acting toward them (*connotative*, sometimes labeled as "behavioral"). Step 3 requires that the items from step 2 be randomized and given to a fairly large number of respondents. The measurement scale is coded into a computer and the results from the scale's items are then submitted to statistical testing (either exploratory factor analysis [EFA] or confirmatory factor analysis [CFA]) to ascertain if the measure "falls out" the same way as the researcher intended.[15] If so, the items that are kept in the scale can be submitted to reliability analysis. If the reliabilities are 0.80 or better (0.70 if the measure will be tested again), then the measure is analyzed to see if it is actually measuring outcomes similar to what should be expected. For instance, if the scale is measuring credibility, how does it correlate to different measures? If there is an event that is being evaluated, do known groups respond as expected? Comparison provides the fourth step of validity—*criterion-related validity*.

Reliability and Validity. As noted earlier, there is a relationship between a measure's reliability and its validity. Obviously a measure that is not reliable will never be valid; however, a valid measure may not be reliable due to problems with the measure's wording or other factors that reduce reliability, such as testing situations, participant language abilities, and so forth.

Extant Measures

How does a public relations professional deal with the 24/7 nature of his job from a measurement perspective, especially with more pressure being placed on him to "demonstrate ROI?" There are hundreds of social variable measures in the academic literature. Delbert Miller's *Handbook* provides multiple measures used in the social sciences and provides background on their development, reliability, and validity.[16] In communication, where nonfinancial indicators relating to credibility, relationship, reputation, and trust abound, there are two excellent sources for measurement scales that can be adapted to whatever the current problem is.[17] Finally, scholarly journals often publish the scales and items employed in published articles and, if not, the authors can be contacted to provide the scales employed in their studies.

Case: The Multiplier Studies

As a case in point, and one that demonstrates that combining academic researchers and professional measurement researchers often produces superior results, we will look at three studies that sought to test the long-held assumption that public relations produced *x* times more outcome than advertising—or a first test of "the multiplier effect."[18] This case was chosen because the authors of this book conducted it and can explain why certain measures were created and the outcomes. The theoretical rationale and study design are available in *Public Relations Journal*;[19] we will focus on the measurement questions and outcomes.

The first study asked a limited number of students to respond to either an advertisement or print editorial copy for one of three products (bottled water, bandage, and flu medication) across four media (print editorial, print advertisement, radio advertisement, web page advertisement) and then evaluate that product as to its credibility (believability) and intent to purchase via a paper-and-pencil self-administered test. These variables were defined initially as traditional business-type forced-choice measures, except that a middle point was added ("neither good nor bad") and respondents who failed to complete an item where coded as "refused to answer." Analyses found no differences across media for any of the three products or for a group who received no stimulus and only the evaluative measures. However, due to the nature of the one-item "measures," we could not be certain if the findings were due to the fact that there was no multiplier effect or respondents marking behavior was unreliable. Further, the study's employment of multiple attitude objects or brands may have impacted the outcomes of interest. Discussion of the study at the 2004 Measurement Summit also pointed out problems with self-administered measures, student populations, and a small number of participants.

Therefore, approaching the revised study as if it were a project for a client (and a client actually came forth and funded the follow-up studies but wished to remain anonymous), we rethought the study from both design and measurement perspectives. The new study differed significantly from what we now called the "pilot study." First, by looking at it as a best practices campaign, we created a new product brand—one that would not have any history or "baggage" attached to it and one that fit into a series of other brands in similar product lines—Zip Chips, a healthy snack. However, we wondered what outcomes would demonstrate a public relations multiplier effect over advertising for a product with no history. A review of marketing and social science literature focused our attention on several nonfinancial outcome variables—credibility, homophily or degree of similarity in an attitude or behavior, brand knowledge, and image—as mediating factors that would predict intent to purchase.

Credibility was further defined as brand authoritativeness and character. Each submeasure was defined by multiple items responded to on a Likert-type "strongly agree" to "strongly disagree" continuum.

The following were credibility statements for authority:

- The product has been presented honestly.
- Based on what I know of it, this product is very good.
- This product is very consumer unfriendly.
- Based on what I know of it, I find this product quite pleasant to use.
- This product is awful.

The following were statements for character:

- Based on what I know of it, this product is an excellent choice for me.
- This product is a value for its price.
- I think this product is very reliable.

The homophily statements were adapted from a measure developed by McCroskey, Richmond, and Daly known as the Perceived Homophily Measure.[20] Homophily measures the degree of similarity between people for an attitude, and in our case was adapted to provide measures of attitudinal and behavioral similarity. All items were responded to on a Likert-type "strongly agree" to "strongly disagree" continuum. Attitudinal homophily was measured on the following items:

- This product is something that is like me.
- People who buy this product are very much like me.
- I would purchase this product because it reflects my lifestyle.

Behavioral homophily was measured on the following items:

- This product is used by people in my economic class.
- This product reflects my social background.
- People who use this product are culturally similar to me.

In addition, participants were asked to compare their knowledge and awareness of the Zip Chip brand against other chip brands. Finally, they were asked a series of questions assessing their knowledge of the brand, how the brand compared to other brands in the same product class, and their intent to purchase Zip Chips.

Three hundred fifty-one shoppers in six malls located in major cities representative of the 48 contiguous United States were randomly selected to participate. All were first screened for age and newspaper readership (the editorial and advertisement were limited to print media). They were then divided into three groups: those exposed to the advertisement, those exposed to the editorial, and a control group who received only the measurement instrument. Instead of reading a testing packet, all participants were interviewed about their attitudes toward Zip Chips by trained interviewers *in situ*. The data were then coded and statistically analyzed. The first analyses were to establish the psychometric validity of the measures and their reliabilities. The results found the measurement scales possessed the expected dimensions, with good or better reliabilities.

The results found no major differences across the study, with the exception of the homophily outcomes, which were significantly higher for those reading the public relations copy than those who saw the advertisement. Further, an analysis of the "don't know" responses to the outcome measures found that those who were exposed to the public relations copy were less unsure of themselves than those exposed to the advertisement copy.

This study was presented in several venues and published on the Institute for Public Relations website. Discussion focused not on the measures, but on the single-stimulus presentation. Therefore a follow-up study using the same outcome measures, but with the advertisement and the print editorial imbedded in a full-page *New York Times* spread, was shown to 651 people at the same six malls. The findings were similar, but of more importance from a measurement perspective, the nonfinancial outcome measures were found to be both reliable and valid.

This case demonstrates that public relations outcomes can be measured and that measuring instruments or scales can be created quite quickly. Further, the basic steps in establishing their validity and reliability can be completed quickly, but only if the measurement researcher has a good understanding of the outcome variables and how they might be adapted to a measurement program within a campaign. The next chapter introduces the concept of secondary research and analysis as a method that helps inform the measurement, assessment, and evaluation process.

Summary

This chapter has taken the reader through the process of creating reliable and valid measures of nonfinancial indicators. It began by setting the stage for public relations measurement that correlates to business outcomes. After a short discussion of the types of variables public relations can measure, it focused on setting up those measures as four different levels of data and discussed what each level adds to our final ROI. The chapter then focused on different kinds of measures appropriate for public relations nonfinancial measurement and ended with a measurement case.

PART II

Qualitative Methods for Effective Public Relations Research, Measurement, and Evaluation

Part II introduces the reader to the gathering of information from a *qualitative perspective*. This perspective is typically employed when the researcher seeks to understand in detail a problem and has no concern with generalizing those findings to a larger audience or population. Part II begins with where all research starts, regardless of the methodologies employed—with what has been researched and reported in the past, also known as *secondary research*. Building upon what has been found through secondary research, which will help in firming up public relations goals and objectives in relation to the larger business goals and objectives, three particular tools of qualitative methodology are explored—*interviews*, *focus groups*, and *participant observation*. Part II ends with an understanding of *content analysis*, a qualitative tool that serves to bridge the qualitative and the quantitative.

CHAPTER 4

Secondary Research

All research methods begin with the gathering of information or data available on a given topic or problem. This gathering of information is called *secondary research*, and although extremely important, may be the most overlooked of the public relations research methodologies available to professionals. Why? In part it may stem from the 24/7 nature of public relations—seldom, it would seem, do public relations professionals have the necessary lead time to conduct *systematic* secondary research on some topic. Second, a great many public relations professionals have little academic coursework in public relations, and a great many have never attempted a research methods course (the perception is that public relations is focused primarily on getting the message out, not evaluating its impact—a perception that by now should be understood as wrong and backward). And, finally, public relations only recently began trying to connect public relations programming to business goals and objectives.

Interestingly, if one looks at public relations budgets as compared to advertising and marketing budgets, very little money by comparison is provided for research; most of that is allocated to the actual collection of campaign data.[1] This, then, begs the question: What do we know about a given topic and where can we gather existing information or data on a particular outcome variable of interest—and how can we do it as cheaply as possible? The answer: Use existing information and data available from the client, from within the organization, or from public documentation found in a variety of places. This is not say that these data will be free, but they will be less expensive than if gathered by one of the methodologies in the following chapters, and they certainly will drive the questions asked when collecting data using other methodologies.

Understanding Secondary Research

Secondary research is the gathering and analyzing of information and data that have already been published in some manner or reside in personal "libraries." Secondary research, then, takes a "second look" at information and data relevant to a particular goal or objective.[2] This information often leads to the creation of personal libraries that contain source material that the public relations professional—or any professional for that matter—will go back to time and time again. Perhaps this volume will become part of the reader's personal library.

What constitutes a library? Materials found in libraries are generally classified into five categories: books, periodicals (newspapers, magazines, professional journals, academic journals), unpublished papers, videos/films, and databases. At one time all would be physically present in the library. In today's libraries, however, with the exception of books (and this is changing as more and more books—like this one—are being "published" as electronic copy), a great majority of these are now filed away electronically. Historically a library was a physical location; today a library can be a physical location, but it can also be accessible to researchers through the Internet or it may reside on special websites.

Case Studies as a Special Category

Case studies, which can include any of the five information sources, are an important element of the public relations library. According to Stacks, public relations case studies can take two forms: historical and strategic (grounded).[3] The most common case study is the historical case. The *historical case study* presents a campaign or research program in a linear fashion, from beginning to end. It assesses what the problem was, the background research, the objectives set, the communication plan put in place, and the evaluation of that plan. The *strategic case study* focuses on strategy and is modeled after case studies found in business. It provides a case history, but does not provide a complete history; instead, it asks the reader to make strategic decisions and then produces what is often called a "teaching note," which evaluates what was done and why it worked or did not. There is a push in the profession for more strategic case studies as public relations professionals are being asked more and more for strategic input into business decisions. Public relations case studies using both the historical and strategic approaches can be found on the Arthur W. Page Society and Public Relations Society of America websites.

Secondary research requires that the researcher have access to it. Although this may sound obvious, many people do not know where to start when they begin to study a problem or are given an objective. Sources of information play an important role in the research program, are located in many places, come in at least three types, have their own validity and reliability, and can be analyzed qualitatively and quantitatively. In this chapter we will examine each not only as part of the methodology, but also as a way of determining which methodologies should be used when collecting data.

Planning to Conduct Research

Although it seems self-evident, planning to conduct research is often an overlooked part of the research program. As noted in chapter 2, the developmental stage of a campaign requires considerable research to define goals and objectives, establish outcomes relevant to those goals and objectives, understand what has been done previously to inform the decision-making process, and choose the appropriate methodologies and analytical approaches. Secondary research is also a vital methodology for choosing measurement systems.

Perhaps one of the most important tasks completed in the development phase of a research program is the stating of questions that will be answered and inform the active research. What secondary research does is provide the researcher with the information necessary to answer four questions relevant to *all* research programs. These questions are typically considered in order, as one informs the next; however, each is singularly important in a research program. We will quickly review the four questions discussed in detail in chapter 1: questions of definition, questions of fact, questions of value, and questions of policy.[4]

Questions of Definition

Since the concern of public relations is to establish that the outcomes of a campaign have met targeted objectives and that these outcomes also correlate to business objectives, it is important that the outcomes be evaluated by data from valid and reliable measures. As noted in chapter 3, measurement, especially measurement that focuses on nonfinancial indicators of success or failure, is heavily dependent on definition. How the outcome variables are defined creates the base for all future research—whether that research focuses on methods or measurement. For instance, what is "trust" in relation to the public relations campaign? Is it the outcome variable (hence it is affected by strategies that target credibility, confidence, reputation, and relationship) or is it one of the variables that public relations focuses on to change perceptions about the product? Further, there are numerous definitions of "trust," just as there are for other nonfinancial indicator variables; some are already defined (termed "reportative," such as those found in the *Dictionary of Public Relations Research and Measurement* or *Communication Research Measures: A Sourcebook*[5]), while others are defined or "stipulated to" in relation to the campaign. Thus "trust" may be defined differently than commonly defined as reflected in the needs of the campaign. Secondary research helps to establish which definitions are relevant to the campaign and which need to be stipulated.

Questions of Fact

Questions of fact follow from the definitions and seek to establish whether the outcome variables do indeed exist. For financial and physical variables, answering a question of fact is quite easy—observe whether the variable exists. For nonfinancial and social variables, the question is not as straightforward or easy to answer. Nonfinancial variables are indicators that, by definition, cannot be "seen." They can be inferred through the measurement of attitudes and beliefs, but their correlation to actual behavior is never 100%. Hence measurement enters into the answer—and measurement instrument or scale reliability and validity are paramount. If you have a reliable and valid measure of the *concept* of "trust" and it correlates well with other demonstrated measures, then you have answered the question of fact. Secondary research provides a history of measures and their reliability and validity as well as cases from previous campaigns to evaluate for effectiveness in measuring what is intended to measure.

Questions of Value

Not all research is factually oriented. Sometimes a researcher is interested in how good or sufficient an outcome is. This involves answering what has been called a "qualitative" question, where the value of something is being evaluated. It may be that the research is more interested in the quality of the responses rather than the number of responses; what was left out of a news release, not what was in it; or the quality of the relationship between important opinion leaders and a product or company. Questions of value answer such questions, and secondary research provides the researcher with an understanding of the communication's value based on previous campaigns and cases.

Questions of Policy

What happens when you kick off a campaign? What information can the researcher find that indicates strategies were appropriate for the problem or client? Questions of policy answer the "should" question: Should the measurement scale be adapted because of audience differences not identified in the developmental stage? Should a different data gathering methodology be employed? Should a different sampling technique be used? Should there be more planned assessment of tactics as the campaign develops? Answers to questions like these are found in being able to look back and evaluate previous research through cases histories and other campaigns. Questions of policy are not typically answered until after the campaign is over and a complete campaign evaluation undertaken; however, secondary research can help answer such questions in advance of the campaign and in its developmental stage.

Benchmarking

It should be clear that secondary research is required when developing the research program supporting a public relations campaign. What secondary research ultimately provides the researcher is a benchmark or series of benchmarks for later comparison during the campaign. It also helps to plan for assessment during the campaign: What methodologies should be used? How many times should data be gathered? What policies should be in place if analysis indicates that objectives are not being met? Too few public relations campaigns actually set benchmarks and then test against them, even though such testing provides a continuous evaluation of a campaign from kickoff to completion. Further, many public relations campaigns cannot address the question of effectiveness because they fail to establish initial benchmarks—baselines—against which to compare results at the campaign's end.

Information Types

What types of information does secondary research seek? In general, there are three types that differ in terms of their authenticity and reliability. All deal with the source of the information. *Primary sources* of information are the actual documents, journal articles, books, news reports, videos, and so forth as produced or printed. They are *it* and there is no question as to interpretation, as they come from the individual or organization that created them. Sometimes primary sources are not available for a number of reasons and we have to rely on *secondary sources*, or reports of the primary source through the eyes of someone else. Without access to the primary source, the researcher needs to ensure that what the secondary source is reporting is what was actually in the primary source. This is often done through cross-referencing of several secondary sources, ensuring that the reporting is reliable and also providing evidence of any bias in the secondary reporting. Finally, there are *tertiary sources*, which are reports of the secondary source. There are times, even with today's Internet accessibility to many information sources, when primary and secondary sources are simply not available. The primary and secondary sources may be confidential reports, may be in restricted access sites, or may simply no longer exist and the researcher is left with a report of a report of a report.

Clearly the goal of anyone conducting secondary research is to gain access to primary sources. When primary sources are not available, secondary sources should be approached with caution and tested for reliability of reporting. Tertiary sources should be examined but rarely used; however, they may provide new avenues to a problem or help if working through definitional problems.

Information Sources

Where does a researcher turn when searching for information while conducting secondary research? Traditionally the answer to that question was easy and clear-cut: the library, or actually "libraries." Today the researcher has a myriad of sources to select from and access to more sources than ever before. This creates a great opportunity, but also is fraught with problems, mainly the ability to establish the reliability and validity of information. Compare a traditional source for beginning secondary research when little is known about the campaign object: a printed encyclopedia such as the *Encyclopedia Britannica* and the electronic encyclopedia, *Wikipedia*. Both are accessible electronically, but only *Britannica* is truly "peer reviewed" (has editors who review the entries for factual errors), while *Wikipedia* allows users to add new entries and edit older entries. *Wikipedia's* advantage of being updated as events change is offset by entries that have been added to promote a particular point of view or are truly wrong. The problem is that with *Wikipedia*, the researcher cannot gauge the accuracy or intent of the entry. In all fairness, *Wikipedia* has tried several workarounds to these problems, but still the researcher can never be sure that the content is accurate, unbiased, or valid. In spite of this, *Wikipedia* can be an excellent starting point, especially when trying to understand a product or client from a contemporary and "up-to-date" perspective.

Traditional Sources

The traditional source for secondary research is the physical library, of which there are two major types: public and private. *Public libraries* are found in almost every city and town in the United States, are open to all, and are the repository of books, magazines, and newspapers (local, national, and sometimes international). There are also libraries that are not open to all; these can usually be found on university and college campuses. These libraries are generally reserved for faculty, students, and other researchers who are given access for "serious" research. They are generally research-oriented but often contain many of the same books, magazines, and newspapers the public library does. In addition, they may have special collections associated only with that particular library.

Private libraries severely restrict access to their holdings. Private universities and colleges often have large holdings, but permission is required for the general public to access them. Still, they are often more accessible than other private libraries, including professional associations, corporations, and personal libraries. Trade association libraries often contain reports and data on a particular sector of the economy and are generally available with little difficulty, but mainly for paid members. Organizational and corporate libraries are much more difficult to access, and access may even be limited within the company to specific people. Many contain confidential reports and sensitive data that the organization does not want made public. Public relations professionals who work for companies should have access to corporate libraries and those working with public relations agencies should have access to information relevant to the problem they have been hired to work on. The final type of library is the personal library. As the name suggests, this is the library of an individual and is usually specific to that individual's interests. Most academics have their own libraries of books and academic and professional journals to aid them with their research. All professionals should build their own working libraries to refer to as they gain expertise in particular areas or for general source material (this book, and others in this series, should be in a personal library).

The preceding discussion should not leave the impression that libraries are no different than they were in the Middle Ages. The modern library is a true repository of information, and almost all libraries are highly interconnected via the Internet so that public access is available without actually ever setting foot in a physical library. What makes the traditional library important, however, is that someone has made decisions on what information is available and checked it out for reliability and validity.

Contemporary Sources

The Internet has opened up secondary research, giving researchers unparalleled access to all types and sources of information. This access, however, does not mean that all sources are valid or reliable. As more and more reputable groups put their information on the Internet, validity and reliability concerns should diminish. Most of what researchers find on the Internet initially comes from search engines, and search engine optimization (SEO) and search engine marketing (SEM) have become hot topics. SEO deals with Internet searches to websites via search engines through unpaid searches; SEM deals with paid Internet searches.[6] Regardless of which path a researcher chooses, working with search engines is no different than using the Dewey decimal system 20 years ago.

Search Engines

Using a search engine takes some thought. A simple search engine query using Google, Yahoo!, and Bing found more than 100,000 possible results for the phrase "public relations." This did not include "PR" as an acronym, which would have yielded even more sites. To use a search engine effectively, the researcher must know exactly what she is looking for—meaning that she has carefully defined what it is she is seeking. Second, it is possible to refine the search using "Boolean operators," terms that help to limit or expand searches. Phrases such as "and," "or," "not," and "else" help the search engine expand or reduce the search. Although not Boolean operators specifically, the use of quotation marks also serves to provide input to the search engine, thus further refining the search. Thus using "public" and "relations" would yield many more than 100,000 results. Also, some search engines allow one to search for specific terms within so many words of each other. For instance, searching for all references to George Walker Bush, knowing they may be "George W. Bush" or "George Bush," helps to refine the search. Third, the results that come up on the computer screen are not always listed by relevance, importance, or even number of times accessed. Companies can pay to have their websites listed early, and if you look at the right side of any search, you will find particular sites that are paid as advertisers. Knowing this and how Boolean operators work makes searching much more efficient.

Although there are many search engines available, some are more central to the secondary research process in that they may be more specialized. For instance, using Bing, Google, or Yahoo! is like using a dictionary or encyclopedia. Factiva and LexisNexis are more media-oriented search engines, as are the search engines associated with major newspapers, such as the *New York Times, Wall Street Journal,* and *Washington Post,* to name but a few "national" newspapers with search engines that allow researchers to access articles from what used to be physical news "morgues." If you want to search for case studies of public relations, advertising, or marketing, you can access Warc (www.warc.com), a site case study website. More specific search engines, such as those searching for medical terms or advice, might include WebMD. Legal questions and findings can be found in Westlaw, if the researcher has access to it. And finally, anyone wanting to search for U.S. government information can use LexisNexis and at least two U.S. government sites: archives.gov or gpoaccess.gov.

Finally, given the popularity of social media—blogs and tweets— search engines have been developed for social media communications. Three top-line search engines are SocialMention, WhosTalkin, and TopRank, with more being developed by the research departments of various public relations agencies.

Databases

Where have search engines come from? Years ago when you wanted to search online for something you went to a database, such as the 1970s HUMRO, which provided one- or two-line notations for mainly unpublished documents that were searched via a series of keywords, such as Shakespeare or Abraham Lincoln. Public relations–specific databases that have developed into powerful websites include the previously mentioned LexisNexis, PR Newswire, Business Wire, Cision, Medialink, and ABI/INFORM.

Assessing Source Reliability and Validity

As noted earlier, much of today's information can be found on the Internet. While the Internet has made access to information easier than ever, it has also made establishing that information's reliability and validity more difficult. Secondary researchers should always be wary of information that comes from the Internet, especially when the website sponsor is not known, is not listed, or has no contact information listed. Assuming that the information appears to come from a credible source, the secondary researcher must then establish its validity and reliability in three subjective ways: content, authority, and through established critical standards.[7] Assessing *content* focuses on answering the following questions positively:

1. Does the content deal with what you need?
2. Does the content match what you already know?

Assessing *authority* focuses on answering the following questions:

1. Who actually wrote the material? What is his/her credibility in the area?
2. Has the material been subjected to editing, fact checking for accuracy, or been submitted to a panel of judges for review prior to publishing?
3. Is the source of the information clearly stated and contact information provided?

Assessing by *critical standards* is more difficult and comes after the information has been read. McCormick suggests the following five questions
be answered:[8]

1. Are the main points and issues clearly identified?
2. Are the underlying assumptions or arguments generally acceptable?
3. Is evidence presented adequate, evaluated clearly, and supportive of
   the conclusions?
4. Is there bias, and is that bias addressed?
5. Is it well written and/or edited?

A second way to assess secondary sources that include data, such as
those found in professional associations or governmental sources, is to
actually conduct statistical tests on those data. As Hocking, Stacks, and
McDermott point out, there are statistical techniques that can be used on
summarized or aggregated data, and if the actual data sets are available,
researchers can run confirmatory tests on the data and compare results to
those that are published and interpreted.[9]

Secondary Research in Measurement and Evaluation

As noted in chapter 3 and earlier in this chapter, secondary research is
particularly important in creating measurement instruments to assess
nonfinancial outcomes, collecting data to check against benchmarks,
and evaluating communication program success. From a best practices
approach, secondary research is essential in carrying out and evaluating a
communication program or campaign. It begins with an ability to understand clients' and products' past experiences, critically evaluate similar
programs through case studies, and find information that can be used as
benchmarks, or if not available, to go into the field to collect that information. Best practices secondary research also dictates what type of data
(qualitative, quantitative, or both) should be collected and how. Further,
it establishes outcome expectations along the campaign timeline that can
be tested against or sets critical benchmarks for testing. Finally, secondary
research provides the research program with the necessary background
against which to conduct final evaluations and to identify and correlate
against other business objectives, including advertising and marketing.

Secondary Research Case

Media Assessment of Saudi Arabia's Reputation and Foreign Perceptions Between September 1, 2007, and November 9, 2007[10]

As part of opening up the Kingdom of Saudi Arabia to the outside world, the Saudis admitted a large number of journalists to cover the Saudi-hosted 2007 Organization of the Petroleum Exporting Countries (OPEC) summit in Riyadh. The Saudi Ministry of Foreign Affairs wanted an international perspective on what the journalists might cover and what effect OPEC's recent oil price increases had on OPEC's reputation and from that prepare anticipatory pointers on how the media agenda might play out.

Echo Research was engaged to conduct secondary research on OPEC, the Kingdom of Saudi Arabia, and worldwide perceptions of both. This secondary research was necessary to prepare Echo's team to establish current perceptions of OPEC and Saudi Arabia, as well as to identify regions of the world, types of media to follow, and potential coding problems. It also sought to identify key opinion leaders and leading analyst companies. The goal was to present the Saudis with strategic recommendations for media relationships and key messaging strategies. The study's objectives were to be able to identify foreign journalists' key concerns, areas where the Saudis and OPEC could expect questions, and potential story areas relating not only to oil but also to stories driven by outside perceptions of Saudi culture.

The study analyzed 584 stories obtained from the general media and social media citizen blogs from the United States, United Kingdom, France, Germany, Spain, Italy, and China—most of the leading economic powers and countries with major interests in OPEC and Saudi oil. This required that the coding of media extracts be done in multiple languages, which added a complication in terms of understanding the meaning of words and phrases. An analysis of secondary data suggested that several areas would be examined, including perceptions of Saudi business, society, government, human rights abuses, and sponsorship of terrorism. Second, they examined perceptions of OPEC, including oil supplies, oil-based economics, and concerns about Middle East stability. In addition, a large "dictionary" of terminology across languages was set up for coder training.

Based on the secondary research, the study produced a number of findings and suggestions. The report found a number of assets and liabilities as seen through the media lens; it identified what it labeled "big, bad issues" that journalists would arrive with and which could drive coverage. This included fringe stories—stories not related to oil—about societal differences and potential misunderstandings based on such factors as treatment of women and a lack of freedom of the press. The study also assessed OPEC from opinion leader analysis and analyst reports, yielding 12 key factors cited for the increase in oil prices.

The study also identified "clusters" of journalists and their reporting on key issues for both Saudi Arabia and OPEC. The clusters were defined by topic and message tone (positive, negative, neutral).

Finally, based on the secondary research's findings, recommendations were made regarding key messaging strategies and strategic media management.

Secondary research played a key role in this study by establishing expectations for events and providing key messaging strategies and media recommendations. Through a thorough search of the existing literature and media stories, Echo was well prepared to conduct the actual gathering of data and subsequent media analysis.

Summary

All public relations practice should begin with secondary research. Best practices require secondary research be as complete as possible. Many times, however, secondary research is overlooked as a major research methodology. Past public relations practices, which did not set benchmarks against which to test for success or failure of public relations efforts, made secondary research seem an afterthought. The 24/7 nature of *reactive* public relations—of tidying up or fixing a crisis—may also figure into the historical lack of secondary research. It should be noted that advertising and marketing programs make secondary research an essential part of their research programs. Contemporary public relations, from a strategic or *proactive* approach, requires that professionals have an understanding of previous research, competitors, and expected business goals and objectives, and continually add to their personal, corporate, and agency libraries secondary materials that can be easily accessed. Contemporary public relations has made this a necessary requirement for best practices.

CHAPTER 5

Qualitative Research Methodologies

Research can take a wide variety of forms, and each of these forms offers unique benefits that can be used to shape and evaluate public relations programs. One of the most basic forms of research is called *qualitative research*. For purposes of describing qualitative research, its applications, and its limitations, it is important to understand what qualitative research is.

The Dictionary of Public Relations Measurement and Research defines qualitative research as "studies that are somewhat to totally subjective, but nevertheless in-depth, using a probing, open ended, response format or reflects an ethno-methodological orientation."[1] Qualitative research differs substantially from quantitative research where the research is "highly objective and projectable, using closed-ended, forced-choice questionnaires; research that relies heavily on statistics and numerical measures."[2]

In essence, qualitative research examines opinions and ideas in depth using the language of a small sample of individuals to explain their representative thoughts, ideas, and reactions to concepts. While this form of research demonstrates the depth and complexity of ideas, it is limited in demonstrating how widely ideas are held among a stakeholder group or a broader population; in other words, its findings are not meant to be generalized beyond the small number of individuals sampled.

The specific value of qualitative research is its ability to provide three key benefits that are not available through other forms of research:

- An understanding of issues in language and perspective of the stakeholder being studied
- Clarification of the findings of quantitative research

- An ability to probe issues to understand the underlying reasons why consumers or others feel the way they do about a particular subject or product

Language and Perspective of the Stakeholder

One of the challenges in conducting almost all forms of research is being able to understand the meaning and intent of the group being studied. This is a classic issue that has confounded social scientists across most disciplines. The work of the anthropologist Clifford Geertz is probably the best example of the *value* of qualitative research. In his 1976 monograph, Geertz argues that in order to truly understand the issues and intentions of the persons or subject under study, it is essential to step outside the perspective of the researcher and attempt to understand the issues or questions from the perspective of and in the language of the observed.[3] This is the central value of qualitative research.

In this form of research, the intent is to present the perspective and consciousness of the observed subjects in conjunction with their own explanation.[4] This explanation and understanding serves as the foundation for preparing questionnaires and other structured research instruments that speak to the respondent of the survey in his or her own language. By using this approach, respondents fully comprehend the question and the intent of the question. In turn, they are able to provide useful and detailed responses with minimal misunderstanding or ambiguity. This procedure increases the validity and reliability of the overall study (see chapter 3).

Clarification of Quantitative Findings and Probing of Issues

One of the primary functions of qualitative research is to assist in the development of larger-scale, quantitative research (see part III). While this is one of the most common uses for qualitative research, there are other applications that can play an essential role in public relations research.

A key attribute of qualitative research is its inherent *flexibility*. The researcher, in working *with* the study participant, is free to explore ideas and concepts that would otherwise be eliminated if a formal and structured questionnaire was used. That is, qualitative approaches allow the respondent in the study to raise issues, questions, and observations with the researcher that normally would not be taken into account if the responses were limited to responding to a standard set of response categories that are shared among everyone participating in the survey. In essence, rather than collecting data, *qualitative research is an iterative process that functions as a dialog between the observed and the observer.*

This flexibility is particularly useful when the researcher needs to understand the underlying issues behind an attitude or a behavior being observed. The central question the researcher is asking at the juncture is "why?": "Why did you buy that product rather than another?" "Why did you vote for that candidate?" or "Why do you like one product more than another?"

The answer to these questions can be used to determine those benefits that influence or modify behavior and can also be used to create communications that are more effective in reaching your goals.

The Application of Qualitative Research

Understanding the application of qualitative research only addresses half the question. It is equally important to understand each of the three qualitative research data collection methods, since each has different applications and each provides unique benefits to the researcher.

The remainder of this chapter will review three popular and widely used forms of qualitative research found in public relations:

- **In-depth interviews**—an informal research method in which an individual interviews another in a one-on-one situation.
- **Focus groups**—an informal research method that uses a group approach to gain an in-depth understanding of a client, object, or product.
- **Participant observation**—an informal research method where the researcher takes an active role in the life of an organization or community, observes and records interactions, and then analyzes those interactions.

The challenge for the public relations researcher is to know which form of qualitative research to use in order to achieve the information objectives for the study. These objectives can include exploratory research to identify issues, pilot studies to explore language and aid in the development of quantitative or structured data collection instruments, confirmatory research used to further explain the "whys" behind quantitative findings, as well as research that can stand on its own.

The Common Elements of All Forms of Qualitative Research

Regardless of the specific method of data collection, each of the three basic forms of qualitative research has common elements that need to be put in place. These common elements include

- defining the objectives for the study;
- determining the decisions that need to be made;
- determining the information needed to make those decisions;
- determining the best source of information;
- identifying the types of respondents or stakeholders who will be included in the study;
- identifying what characteristics or attributes they have in common;
- identifying what products they use;
- identifying their shared attitudes or behaviors;
- obtaining lists or other sample sources that can be used to identify specific individuals who meet the criteria to qualify as respondents for the study and possibly be included as participants;
- preparing data collection instruments or interview guides that will assist the interviewer in conducting interviews that are consistent across the entire sample and ensure the information objectives for the study are met;
- conducting the interviews in a manner that will ensure open and honest responses;
- analyzing the interviews in order to reach clear conclusions and recommendations that address the information objectives for the study.

Sample Sources

Although chapter 7 addresses sampling in detail, it is important to understand that the sources for the samples to be included in qualitative research can vary widely. These sources can be as simple as a list of employees of a company or as complex as individuals who share an unusual preference, attitude, or behavior toward a product or service. Further, those chosen for the sample need not be selected at random; qualitative researchers have an advantage in that they can target specific individuals due to their status, importance, or other characteristics.

Types of lists that can be used include registered users of products, specialized directories, subscription lists, and warranty lists. These lists are available from list brokers and focus group facilities, as well as from clients who may have collected this information for other purposes. The information on these lists includes the name of the individual being recruited and contact information, as well as any information that may be relevant in the decision to ask for their cooperation in the study.

Recruiting Respondents for Study Participation

Recruiting respondents for a study can be accomplished in a variety of ways that are as diverse as the types of respondents who are likely to participate in this type of research. For example, executive interviews are often arranged through a client or third party that has knowledge of the project but also has a direct relationship with the potential respondent. In these circumstances, the respondent knows the purpose of the research and has a direct stake in the outcome. However, the typical qualitative research project requires a more complex process in order to ensure the objectives of the study are met.

In many qualitative research projects, respondents are not selected for *who* they are. Rather they are included in the study for *what* they do or prefer, *where* they live, *when* they do things, or *why* they might engage in specific activities. The process for identifying these potential respondents is called *screening*. Typically the screening process is based on a questionnaire. The questionnaire asks a series of questions that are designed to ensure that the participants in a qualitative study exactly match the specifications for the project. This ensures that the objectives for the study are met.

The typical screening questionnaire usually takes less than 5 minutes to administer and can ask about product use or ownership, personal demographic or household characteristics, intended behaviors, attitudes, or preferences. In many instances, the questions are written in a manner that "masks" the intent or focus of the study so that respondents participating in the project are unaware of the actual intent or focus of the study. For example, if the focus of the study is wristwatches, it is likely the respondents will also be asked about other products as part of the screening process (e.g., rings, necklaces, earrings). This procedure is followed so that respondents do not have preconceived attitudes or biases based on their prior knowledge. It also helps to ensure that respondents provide honest responses during the interview.

In addition to these screening items, the questionnaire also includes detailed information about when and where the interview will take place and what, if any, compensation may be provided in exchange for their cooperation. These "incentives" are typically only used for consumer or general public research and some limited business-to-business applications. For consumers or the general public, a fee of between $40 and $50 is often offered. In contrast, senior executives, physicians, and other hard to reach audiences may be offered incentive payments of several hundred dollars in exchange for their cooperation and assistance. However, incentives or other gifts are inappropriate for qualitative research among employees or among those that have a direct interest in the outcome of the research.

Discussion or Interview Guide

Once the study participants are recruited, it is essential to make sure that the data collection matches the objectives of the research, which should reflect the business objectives of the internal or external client, and that the interviews are conducted *consistently*. However, since the questions are typically open-ended in qualitative research, it becomes more challenging to design than structured data collection instruments such as questionnaires. Structured questionnaires are commonly designed around specific questions that have a predefined set of potential answers. These answer categories can be as simple as "yes" and "no" or can be as complex as scaled questions that ask the degree to which someone agrees or disagrees with a concept or idea (see chapter 3).[5] Qualitative research, however, requires a much more flexible approach that allows the interviewer *and* the study participant opportunities to expand upon their questions and answers, exploring concepts and ideas that may arise in the course of the interview.

The process that is used in this type of interview is called *open-ended interviewing*. An open-ended interview asks the following questions:

- "Please describe how you use the product or service."
- "What do you think of the candidate?"

These questions are often supplemented with probes that get at the underlying reasons behind why a position is held. *Probes* typically include these follow-up questions:

- "Why do you feel that way?"
- "Would you give me an example?"
- "Can you elaborate on that idea?"
- "Could you explain that further or give more detail?"
- "I'm not sure I understand what you're saying."
- "Is there anything else that will help me to understand?"

The interview typically starts with a broad, general discussion on a topic that leads into questions that become increasingly specific. This approach introduces the topic of the interview to the respondents, who typically start by commenting on their more general attitudes or experiences. This stage of the interview is designed to set the context of how respondents use a product or service or understand a situation. This context is used to set the stage for the remainder of the interview, which asks more specific questions.

It is also important to note that it is the responsibility of the interviewer to fully disclose why the research is taking place and how the findings will be used. This discussion does not have to be specific, nor does the client or the sponsoring organization need to be identified. A typical explanation could include, "This study is being done to understand consumer reaction to a new product. The findings of the study will be used to help develop a better advertisement."

Respondents also need to be assured that their responses are confidential and anonymous; that is, that their names will not be associated with the findings, nor will their responses be reported in ways that could potentially identify them—something that is extremely important in getting responses that are genuine, allowing respondents to be candid and open in their responses. If the session is being recorded, it is also essential to disclose this to the study participants and to let them know that the recording will only be used to aid the research team in the analysis.

These are the common elements of each of the three basic forms of qualitative research. It is the role of the researcher to determine which of these three types of interviewing methods is most appropriate for the study at hand.

In-Depth Interviews

In-depth interviews are the most researcher controlled of the qualitative methods. These interviews are generally conducted one on one and the researcher has more control over respondent answers to questions than in the other two qualitative methods.

When to Use In-Depth Interviews

In-depth interviews are most effective when it is necessary to interview study respondents who fall into one of the following categories:

- Senior-level or difficult to reach individuals who are unlikely to have flexible schedules and are therefore unlikely to be willing or able to participate in a group study
- Respondents or study participants who are widely and geographically dispersed
- When comments or input from another study participant, or even being in the same room with another participant, would influence or inhibit candid or honest responses

- When it is necessary to re-create an environment where the respondent is exposed to concepts and ideas in a "natural" setting, such as reading a magazine or watching television

The process for conducting the research follows the qualitative research guidelines that cover sampling, recruiting, and the types of questions asked, as well as the general research principles of defining the stakeholders or respondents for the research, determining what information is needed, and soliciting the cooperation of the respondents asked to participate in the research.

Focus Groups

The focus group, often called a "controlled group discussion," removes some of the control over the research session. In the focus group, a moderator (sometimes the researcher) asks predetermined questions to a group of recruited individuals and exercises control through nonverbal eye contact or direct questions to specific members once a dialogue within the focus group has been achieved, typically drawing out reticent participants or probing for more or different responses.

When to Use Focus Groups

The greatest value of focus groups is having stakeholders with a shared or common background or interest exchange ideas on a product, service, or activity. The broad objective of this type of research is to have the group explore the diversity of opinion on a topic and to provide feedback on concepts and ideas that take that diversity into account.

One of the most common applications of focus groups is to test communications programs. These programs include simple copy tests, where respondents are exposed to advertising or press materials and are asked to determine what they learned as well as how effective the materials are in communicating intended ideas. Other applications include exploration of attitudes to assist in creating structured surveys, clarification of survey findings, and reactions to events or spokespersons. In each instance, the groups are exploring how respondents feel about a topic, why they hold that opinion, and how their opinions differ or converge from their peers.

Participant Recruitment

Most focus groups are recruited through professional services that specialize in this type of service. These "recruiters" rely on structured "screener" questionnaires. Screeners can cover a wide variety of topics and are typically "masked," so the purpose or topic of the focus group is not revealed in advance to the respondents. This precaution is taken so that respondents provide "top-of-mind" responses. These responses are generally considered to be more open and honest since they are not preconditioned, that is, responses that the respondent believes the moderator or other observers want to hear.

The typical screener will initially ask about product, service, or activity use and may include specific questions about brands used or considered. Attitudinal questions may also be asked in addition to product, service, or activity questions. These questions are often supplemented with demographic questions that can be used to create the desired profile of the group. For example, in some instances it is preferable to have an even mix of men and women in a group session. In other instances, men and women might be in separate groups, particularly if it is perceived that gender plays a role in shaping opinions. This separation is done to encourage open dialogue among peers, as well as to provide groups that are easier to compare and contrast. Other types of demographic considerations around which groups may be organized are age (younger and older), education, or marital status.

The final section of the screening interview is an invitation to attend the group. The invitation provides a brief description of a general topic, when and where the group will meet, and the compensation the respondent might expect to receive for participation. As noted earlier, this compensation can range from as little as $40 to as much as several hundred dollars, depending on the type of respondent and the location or city where the group takes place.

Discussion Guide

The discussion or interview guide for a focus group follows the same structure that is used for an individual in-depth interview. The only difference that needs to be considered is group dynamics. Questions should be structured to encourage dialogue *between* participants in the focus group as well as uncover the diversity of opinion on a topic. These types of questions may include "What are other people's opinions on this topic?" "Why do you feel differently about that?" or "Are there any other ways of thinking about this?"

Probing questions also need to be included that encourage this type of interchange. These probes can include questions such as "Why do you feel that way?" "How did you reach that conclusion?" or "What motivated you to make that decision?" These types of questions get at the foundations of the issues by looking at motivations and rationales that can be used to understand behaviors and preferences. This understanding is often used to develop the core messages and language of effective communications programs.

Moderator

Group interviewing requires very specific skills that differ considerably from those required for individual in-depth interviews. Consequently, it is strongly recommended that any research project requiring focus groups consider a professionally trained individual who has specific experience with this type of data collection method. However, the selection of a moderator often requires much more than experience with group interviews. Careful consideration also needs to be given to their experience with the topic or product category, the objectives of the research, and the nature of the respondents participating in the group interview.

An example where a moderator with specific skills or background would be considered is for a pharmaceutical product targeted to older women. In this instance, it is important for the moderator to be conversant on pharmaceutical products as well as have the ability to communicate with the respondents in an open manner that encourages frank discussion and interchange. In this instance, it is highly likely that a middle-age or older female moderator would be the best choice for conducting the interviews.

Interviewing Room

The location of the focus group needs careful consideration. In general, the following need to be considered when deciding on a location and arranging a focus group room:

- The room should be a conference or seminar room with a large table that seats 10 interview participants, as well the moderator. Preferably the seating in the room should be arranged as in Figure 5.1.
- Name cards with names should be available for each participant. These can be prepared with card stock and markers.
- Recording equipment should be available. A stationary compact video camera that can be mounted on a tripod works very well. The tripod should be placed behind and above the moderator or behind a viewing mirror in order to get a full view of the participants. Table-level omnidirectional microphones will help ensure better sound quality, but this is not a necessity.
- Assuming a mirrored viewing room is not available, and if a second room is available nearby or next door, you may want to have a video monitor available so observers can watch the groups live.
- Beverages or light snacks should be available, as focus group sessions can last up to 2 hours and this will help increase participation in the groups.

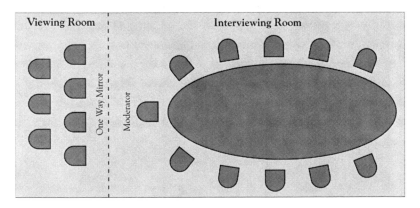

Figure 5.1. Focus group room arrangement.

General Specifications for All Group Recruitment

The number and diversity of respondents is an important consideration when planning a focus group. In general, the following are true:

- Groups are most productive with 8 to 10 respondents participating. You should try to avoid overrecruiting if possible.
- Diversity is important in focus group studies in order to explore the widest possible range of opinions. This diversity may include age, gender, or various types of product use. However, in order to aid in the analysis, you may want to organize groups so they are homogeneous. This will encourage shared opinions, as well as a willingness to be open. An example where this is important is on sensitive personal issues, such as financial issues or sexuality.
- If multiple groups are scheduled for a single time period, the groups should be scheduled with a break of 15 to 30 minutes between sessions. This will allow the moderator to collect his/her thoughts and prepare for the next session.

An important consideration is the number of groups scheduled for a given study. Generally two or more groups should be scheduled if funding allows. This allows the researcher to establish if responses, although subjective, are similar between the two groups and helps in the final evaluation of the focus group study. When homogeneous groups are planned, say male-only and female-only groups discussing sex, researchers can establish not only the reliability of group responses, but also differences between the groups.

Participant Observation

Participant observation offers researchers the least amount of control over data collection. Concerns about participant observation as a method arise when people are unobtrusively observed going about their daily activities, which is one form of participant observation often found in academic settings.[6] The form suggested in this volume differs in that the observation is not unobtrusive, but instead takes place within environments wherein the respondents actually live, work, or socialize.

When to Use Participant Observation

Participant observation is a research method borrowed from cultural anthropology. In this method, also sometimes referred to as *ethnography*, "the researcher takes an active role in the life of an organization or community, observes and records interactions, and then analyzes those interactions."[7] The data collection method tries to understand "how individuals and groups function in their natural settings."[8] Consequently the most appropriate use of this method is to gain an understanding of how individuals and groups actually use or interact with a product, service, or activity and how that product, service, or activity fits into their day-to-day lives.

This type of research has been applied to a wide variety of settings and applications, including consumer products, as well as to corporations in order to gain an understanding of how individuals interact with products, their environment, and each other.

The Interview

Unlike other forms of qualitative research, there is less structure and the questions are flexible to reflect that each participant in the study lives or works in a different environment. The interviewer spends a considerable portion of the interview observing how the product, service, or activity is engaged or interacted with. Questions are asked not about what the respondent is doing, but instead, the questions focus on why they choose to engage in specific interactions and how they became involved.

Like other forms of qualitative research, these interviews and observations are often recorded using both audio and video equipment. Video recording becomes particularly important because significant portions of the data collection are observation rather than the interrogative forms used in other forms of qualitative research.

One of the primary features of the participant observation interview is that the data collection period is often long and very open-ended. Observations can be as short as a few minutes or can often extend for days, depending on the nature of the observation, the type of respondent, and the overall objectives of the research. Consequently participant observations typically rely on a very limited number of interviews, using

Table 5.1. Comparing the Three Forms of Qualitative Research

Benefit	In-Depth Interviews	Focus Groups	Participant Observation
Involvement of challenging or difficult to reach respondents	✓		
Ability to ask in-depth questions	✓	✓	✓
Interaction and exchange of ideas		✓	
Concept testing	✓	✓	
Understanding actual product, service, or activity use			✓

sample sizes that are considerably smaller than other forms of qualitative research. In many instances, this type of study may consist of no more than a handful of independent observations.

The Interviewer

The skills required for participant observation research differ considerably from those used in other forms of qualitative research. It is important for the researcher to take note of product use as well as interactions with the overall environment. Questions are used to supplement these observations and often have to be developed during the course of the interview.

Case Study: Assessing Employee Attitudes Toward Change After Coming out of Chapter 11 Bankruptcy in the Energy Sector[9]

What happens to employee attitudes toward senior management after new management takes a formerly regulated company out of bankruptcy and instills a new vision and mission? This question was asked by a large energy company in the late 1990s. Research into the company revealed that it was a poorly run, large company dominant in one geographic region and a company that focused primarily on the delivery of energy products to business and residential customers. The company filed for bankruptcy just prior to the energy deregulation legislation of the 1980s and was brought out of bankruptcy by a young chief executive officer (CEO) in the mid-1990s under an umbrella structure of central administration and 16 other energy-related subsidiaries ranging from energy development, to transportation, to delivery.

About 5 years after bankruptcy the senior vice president for human resources, in conjunction with the CEO, requested an outside set of consultants to provide an assessment of employee perceptions of the company's new mission and vision, which stressed the safe, reliable delivery of inexpensive energy. To meet this new company vision and mission, employees were asked to work harder and more efficiently. The consultants, after conducting as much secondary research as possible about the company and the "new" energy industry and having conducted several earlier studies on the company's media coverage and employee perceptions of communication tools, created a questionnaire and conducted a random survey of employees. These surveys were weighted to represent the 16 subsidiaries and umbrella organization and yielded slightly more than 400 responses that were in line with subsidiary and umbrella employee percentages of the total population. The findings delivered rather bleak news—new employees reported low morale and communications, older employees felt betrayed and that newer employees did not understand the industry; all employees felt, in spite of a large new home office building replete with all the computerized bells and whistles available at that time, that senior management was going to sell them out.

The survey, while instructive, could not answer the "how well," "how much value," or "why" questions that seemed to plague responses. Further, the consultants were unable to interview senior management, subsidiary leadership, and union leaders, with the exception of the human resources and communications senior vice presidents, who were now responsible for the study (the CEO removed himself from the study, asking only for a final report). It was agreed that the consultants would take the survey results and conduct a series of focus groups among the subsidiaries and the umbrella office. Because of costs, a limited number of focus groups were run (14 in 7 locations) and only two 2-hour groups per physical area were conducted. Within each focus group, respondents were invited to participate such that all levels of the organization were represented among the 10 to 12 participants—from fuel truck operators to vice presidents. The proportion of males to females was calculated based on data provided by human resources, and all participants were guaranteed confidentiality and anonymity. In only one group was there a problem with a senior manager as a respondent, and he removed himself from the focus group at break time.

The results confirmed the survey findings and more. The CEO, who used to frequently travel between subsidiaries and walk the hallways to discuss business and other things with employees, had locked himself in his glass-walled office and had increased the number of administrative assistants, resulting in reduced personal visibility. Further, the CEO's profile had risen across the energy industry while he had reduced contact with employees. Employees were consistent across all focus groups in their perceptions and attitudes that the vision and mission, while something to strive for, was not where time and money were being spent. Indeed, one group had done further investigation into the CEO's background and noted that he stayed, on average, 5 years with a company he brought out of bankruptcy before selling it and moving on.

The focus groups provided a vast amount of information that could have been used to increase internal communications and a number of suggestions on how to better meet the company's new vision and mission statements. A report was written and submitted. Approximately 1 year later the company was bought out by another energy company . . .

Limitations of Qualitative Research

Qualitative research has unique benefits that are unavailable from other forms of data collection. It is flexible and adaptable. It gets at underlying issues. It probes for the "whys" behind the "whats." However, even with these benefits, qualitative research is not appropriate in every instance.

The three primary limitations are that qualitative research is (1) costly, (2) time consuming and labor intensive, and (3) cannot be used to reliably measure or determine the extent to which attitudes, opinions, or behaviors are held or engaged in by a particular population.

The costs of qualitative in-depth interviews can often exceed $1,000 per interview when preparation and analysis time are taken into consideration. Added to the fact that data collection can take a considerable amount of time to complete, the overall number of interviews included in qualitative research is often quite limited. This makes it difficult to extrapolate the results to a broader population. However, when used in combination with surveys, qualitative research is a powerful tool for effective and useful communications research.

CHAPTER 6

Content Analysis

Content analysis is one of the most commonly used, and at the same time misused, public relations measurement and evaluation tools. Because it is often considered the most basic form of public relations measurement, content analysis is frequently seen as a less-effective and less-reliable form of public relations measurement and evaluation. However, when used properly, content analysis can be critical in evaluating overall communications effectiveness and function to help plan more effective public relations and media relations strategies.

This chapter explores several key aspects of content analysis, starting with a basic understanding of the nine types of public relations content analysis that are commonly used. It also explores alternative approaches that can be used in conjunction with other forms of research as an essential tool in an overall public relations measurement and evaluation toolkit.

Understanding the Basics of Content Analysis

Before we look at the specific forms of content analysis, we need to first examine the basic steps anyone using these nine types of analysis must take. While content analysis appears to be a very basic and straightforward research method, it is more complicated than it seems and must be approached in a systematic manner that requires the researcher to make informed decisions at each step of the research process.

Determining the Analytic Framework

As with any sound research method, the researcher should begin by examining what has been done before by conducting, at least informally, a secondary or historical review of similar studies or cases. This provides the researcher with information that is necessary to establish what will be evaluated as part of the content analysis. This includes (1) which messages, (2) the priorities of those messages, (3) how to classify and count the messages or parts, and (4) how to establish whether the coding is reliable and the competitive framework for the analysis. This analysis is compiled into a document often referred to as a "code sheet," which lists all the issues and messages as well as competitors that are included as part of the overall study.

For a more complete review of the analytical framework, see the *Primer of Public Relations Research.*[1]

Selecting the Message Pool

If content analysis is conducted on all messages that are obtainable in a given set of articles, then the message pool or population results in a census of all messages. However, in many instances, obtaining all messages is not practical because many of the messages are not directly relevant to the business issues at hand. Consequently it is common practice that some type of selective sampling of these messages be completed. These messages can be determined in two ways. The first approach is to review a sample of articles to determine which messages or issues are common across the articles. The second approach is to determine these messages "a priori," that is, independently of what is actually written. The messages used in the analysis are those that are typically important to the recipient of the study. In practice, message selection is a hybrid approach that actually uses both of these methods in an iterative combination of hypothesis testing and evaluation in order to obtain a final list.

Establishing the Unit of Analysis

Once your message pool has been established, content analysis requires a definition of what is being analyzed. This is called establishing the unit(s) of analysis. The unit of analysis can take several forms—and often more than one is established for analysis. The unit of analysis defines what is being analyzed and is generally of two types.[2] *Manifest* units of analysis are *what can be seen*: words, pictures, names, spatial calculations, and so forth. *Latent* units of analysis are *what must be inferred* from the content:

accuracy, tone, and indicators of liking, violence, and so forth. The unit of analysis is carefully defined and then pretested to ensure that coders (those who will actually review each message and decide how the unit of analysis is to be interpreted) are evaluating the same content the same way.

Establishing Category Systems

Once the unit of analysis has been defined and tested, the next step is to create a category system. The category system is where you will place your units of analysis as they are evaluated. This is often referred to as coding, but in actuality, what is coded is dependent on the category system created. There are several rules for establishing categories.

First, the *categories must reflect the purpose of the research*. That is, if our study is on company X's reputation, then categories should include reputational units of analysis, so a category on auto racing would not reflect the purpose (unless the company had an affiliation with racing).

Second, *the categories must be exhaustive*. The content must be put in a category; it cannot be left out. This leaves the ubiquitous category "other" as a catch-all. Best practice content analysis always pretests the category system on randomly selected content before conducting a full-fledged analysis to ensure the categories are exhaustive. As a rule of thumb, when the "other" category reaches 10%, the category system should be reexamined. Sometimes events may occur that require the addition of new categories. Theoretically the content should be recoded, taking into account the new category, but in practice, a note is made and the other categories are compared before and after this point in time.

Third, *categories must be independent of each other*—that is, something cannot be put in one because it is not in another; the content must fit by definition, although as noted above, sometimes events force new categories. For instance, at one time you could categorize football and basketball positions by a player's jersey number. Today a point guard can wear the number 50 or 1; the same is true in football, where almost all linemen had jerseys with numbers between 50 and 70 but now some wear jerseys with numbers between 80 and 90.

Finally, *all categories must represent one classification system.* As noted earlier, categorizing athletes by jersey number for position, while problematic today, is a classification system. If the content analysis were to have a second system, say jersey color, then confusion might occur and the classification system might yield error in placing content in the correct category. This can affect the validity and reliability of the analysis (see chapter 3).

Coding

This step should be the easiest once the unit(s) of analysis and category system have been put in place. Coding requires that someone trained in the content make decisions about the categorizing of the content. Coders should be carefully trained to (1) understand the unit of analysis being coded and (2) place that content in the appropriate category. All coders (ranging from one to several) should practice coding the data until minimal coding errors are obtained.

Establishing Coding Reliability

Coding reliability tells the researcher how much error occurs in coding judgment. While 100% coding reliability is the goal, there is *always* some coding error. During coder training, reliability estimates of coding should be conducted until coders are in agreement at least 90% of the time.[3] After the coding has been completed, a final reliability test should be run using either Holsti's reliability coefficient or Scott's *pi* statistic.[4] Holsti's coefficient is a general reliability estimate and is quite easy to hand calculate, while Scott's *pi* is much more difficult to compute, but is much more conservative. Most computerized content analysis programs now include both.

Approaches to Content Analysis

Content analysis takes many different forms, with each form measuring and evaluating very different aspects of a public or media relations program or campaign. Overall there are nine distinct types of content analysis commonly used in public relations, with many methods being combined into unified or composite analyses. The nine types of content analysis can be further divided into three general categories based on what is actually coded:

- No Message Evaluation
  - Clip Counting
  - Circulation and Readership Analysis
  - Advertising Value Equivalence (AVE)

- Manifest Message Evaluation
  - Simple Content Analysis
  - Message Analysis

- Latent Message Evaluation
  - Tonality Analysis
  - Prominence Analysis
  - Quality of Coverage
  - Competitive Analysis

As a first step in reviewing the application of content analysis in public relations measurement and evaluation, we will review how each of these nine types of analysis are typically applied in public relations.

No Message Evaluation

There are three basic approaches to content analysis in public relations that do not deal with message evaluation—clip counting, circulation and readership analyses, and advertising value equivalency.

Clip Counting

This is the most basic—and perhaps most antiquated—form of content analysis used in public relations. With this system, relevant articles are collected and typically sorted chronologically. The analysis generally consists of a summary listing the publications and dates of publication as well as the total article count. Typically these clips are bound together in chronological volumes. One of the most common analyses used in combination with clip counting is the "thud factor," or the overall volume of noise generated when the book of bound press clippings hits or "thuds" against a table or other flat surface.

The analysis contains no insights, discussion of, or interpretation of the coverage and is dependent on the recipient of the report to draw judgments about the actual content. These judgments are generally qualitative, usually based on reading a handful of articles, articles that may or may not typify the actual coverage a media relations effort actually received.

Circulation and Readership Analysis

The next level of content analysis builds upon clip counting by adding information about each article that is gathered from secondary data sources. These sources typically include BurrellesLuce (provides press-clipping services that also include circulation information and other third-party information about the article), Nielsen Research (provides television audience measurement and related services used to determine audience size and composition for broadcast and cable programming), Arbitron (a media and marketing research firm that measures audiences for radio and other media services), Scarborough (a provider of readership information for local and national newspapers), Audit Bureau of Circulations (ABC; a third-party organization that audits and certifies the circulation of print publications), Simmons Market Research Bureau (SMRB), and Mediamark Research (MRI; national surveys of consumers that measure consumer purchases as well as consumer media habits). These surveys are commonly used as tools for planning media purchases by advertisers.

The specific types of information added to a clip counting analysis may include circulation of the publication or the number of printed or "hard" copies distributed, total readership or the total number of actual readers (circulation multiplied by the average number of readers for each copy), demographic profiles of the readership of each publication (e.g., age, gender, income, education), and possibly even product use, attitudinal, lifestyle, or psychographic information.

A common approach with this type of analysis is to present a total circulation or total readership that is the total number of copies distributed or the total number of individuals who are likely to have read a given copy. Total readership is also referred to as "pass along" or gross readership.

However, these approaches can be further modified to include only "qualified" readers—those readers who are of specific interest to the evaluator. An example of a qualified reader is a particular gender or age group to whom a public relations program is directed (e.g., men 18 to 34 years old, college graduates, military officers, etc.) Actual analysis of the content of the articles, however, is not part of the study.

Advertising Value Equivalence

Advertising value equivalence is an estimate of the cost to purchase advertising that has an equivalent size and location in a given publication on a specific day. These estimates are typically based on information provided by the Standard Rate and Data Service (SRDS), which is a database of media rates and information that is used by advertising agencies. This approach is discredited by many public relations professionals as well as by leading researchers as it is primarily based on the assumption used in many advertising value analyses that a public relations placement is worth more than or is a multiple of an equivalent advertisement in its overall impact or effect. However, recently published work demonstrates that advertising and public relations are likely to be equally effective at communicating similar messages.[5] While there are some applications where AVEs may have some limited utility, this approach is generally considered flawed.[6]

As in the analysis of circulation or readership, actual analysis of the content of the articles is not included in this type of study.

Manifest Message Evaluation

Manifest message evaluation takes two forms: simple content analysis and message analysis.

Simple Content Analysis

This is a simple analysis that classifies or codes what is written into categories that can, in turn, be statistically analyzed. The categories or codes are developed by a close textual analysis of a small sample of randomly selected articles, often as few as 10%. The remaining articles are analyzed based on the presence of these codes. Each article is read to determine the presence of specific pieces of information that is classified according to the codes. Information from the codes is then entered into a database to determine the frequency of codes or classifications of information.

Because this approach is based on the presence of specific codes or categories, this method accurately represents only what is actually written. Intended messages or specific items of information that are not included in the codes or do not appear in the articles are not included in the analysis. This method also does not draw inferences about the accuracy or desirability of the information included in the articles.

Coding is commonly done using readers who have been specifically trained to perform this task. This approach is limited by the potential fallibility and inconsistency of the readers responsible for the coding. To address this challenge, many organizations that code or classify the content of news articles limit the number of readers to just a handful. This use of a limited number of readers ensures consistency and results in a higher degree of "intercoder reliability," that is, "the extent to which the different judges tend to assign exactly the same rating to each object."[7]

In the past few years, computerized systems have been developed to address these issues. However, these systems tend to be inflexible and often miss articles or misclassify the results. While significant advances have been made in this area, the most accurate coding is still conducted using human readers.

Message Analysis

Message analysis differs from simple content analysis by centering the analysis on the presence of intended messages in articles. Key messages are developed based on communication objectives (see chapters 1 and 2). These communication objectives are "translated" into codes that become the basis of the analysis. Articles are coded by the presence of key messages included in each article. The analytic process is similar to a simple content analysis, where the codes from each article are entered into a database for statistical analysis. Message analysis, however, is still limited in its overall scope because it only includes the presence or absence of specific messages. The accuracy and completeness of messages is not part of the overall analysis.

Latent Message Evaluation

Latent message evaluation currently takes four forms and is the direction in which content analysis is moving. The four forms are tonality analysis, prominence analysis, quality of coverage, and competitive analysis.

Tonality Analysis

Tonality analysis uses a subjective assessment to determine if the content of an article is either favorable or unfavorable to the person, company, organization, or product discussed in the text.

There are a variety of different ways to assess tone. One of the most common is a simple classification of "positive," "neutral," or "negative." Other approaches rate each article or code on a finite scale, such as "0 to 100" scale where "0" is completely negative and "100" is completely positive. An example of this type of scale is one used by Echo Research (see Figure 6.1). That scale (0 to 100) takes into consideration a number of criteria when evaluating an article. These criteria include where in the publication an article is placed, the

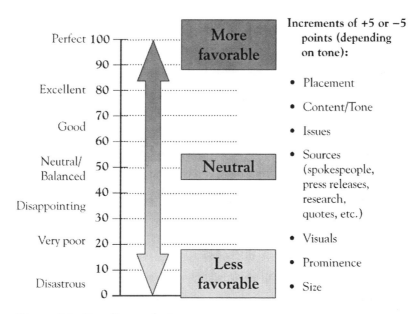

Figure 6.1. Tonality analysis.
Used with permission of Echo Research.

overall content and tone of the article, which issues and messages are included in the article, sources cited, the use of visuals, as well as the overall prominence and size of the article.

Other options include scales with positive and negative ratings. An example is a scale with a rating of "–50" to "+50." In this instance, "–50" is completely negative and "+50" is completely positive. A neutral analysis would be recorded as "0" on this scale.

This method can be applied using several different approaches. The first is an assessment of the tonality of the overall article. Other approaches assess the tone of a specific mention or code the tone of a specific message that may appear in an article. Each article is typically assessed individually and the findings can be aggregated to present an overall assessment of the tone of the media.

Prominence Analysis

Prominence analysis accounts for six factors: (1) the publication where the article appears, (2) the date of appearance, (3) the overall size of the article, (4) where in the publication it appears, (5) the presence of photography or other artwork, (6) and the size of headlines. In a typical prominence analysis, each element is given a weight that is factored into an overall score for each article. That score determines the prominence of the article.

Certain publications (e.g., *New York Times* or *Wall Street Journal*) are generally rated as having higher prominence than others. This assessment is generally based on the size and perceived quality of the readership. The date of appearance can also be a factor because readership can be much higher on specific days (e.g., Sunday or Monday).

In this analysis, articles that receive higher prominence scores are given more emphasis in the evaluation since it is assumed that higher readership, prominence of the publication, size and placement of the article, or a combination of these factors leads to higher communications effectiveness. The limitation of this approach is that prominence is typically a highly subjective measure. There are no reliable methods to ensure that prominence is rated consistently from publication to publication or from evaluator to evaluator. This often results in inconsistency of results, thus making it difficult to compare results over time.

Recent efforts have attempted to develop an objective measure for article prominence. Some of these "objective" measures of prominence rely on an advertising value equivalency model that assumes that a high AVE reflects both the prominence of the publication (e.g., quality of audience) and the size of the placement as well as the location (e.g., cover page, center page, back page, etc.) of the article within the publication. However, there is not yet any conclusive research that validates the use advertising rates as a proxy for determining article placement.

Quality of Coverage

Quality of coverage is often based on a combination of factors. The factors typically included in this measure are tonality (positive, neutral, or negative), prominence, placement, the inclusion of specific messages in the article, as well as the overall volume of articles generated. Each of these factors is entered into a computation that generates a score for each individual article in the analysis. This generates a "quality of coverage score" that is similar to the scales discussed earlier in this chapter. However, many of these elements are highly subjective and are subject to the interpretation of the reader. The most significant limitation of this approach is that the evaluation is typically not tied to the outcomes that are anticipated from the public relations efforts. Therefore, while "quality" is assessed, the impacts of the messages placed are not taken into consideration.

Competitive Analysis

In addition to the analysis of an individual topic, event, brand, or company, a content analysis can also be conducted comparing the performance of companies, brands, topics, or events with their media coverage. This can range from comparisons of the total number of clips to comparisons of the overall prominence one brand or company receives over another. This is often used as a way to assess relative performance in the media as well as identify where gaps exist and where there may be opportunities for further or enhanced communications efforts.

Other variations of content analysis exist, many of which use proprietary systems and employ a combination of the techniques previously discussed.[8]

The Challenge of Traditional Approaches to Content Analysis

As widely available and diverse as each of these methods of content analysis are, public relations practitioners rarely make use of even the most rudimentary of these research methods. The only exception is the high prevalence of clip counting—a method of content analysis that is almost universally applied among public relations consultants and their clients.

Even when a content analysis is conducted, the evaluation rarely, if ever, offers any insights more profound than the tonality of placements (e.g., positive, neutral, or negative). Consequently these analyses fail to offer diagnoses of the situation or prescribe a solution that is tied to communications objectives.

We can speculate on the reasons for this lack of acceptance of one of the most basic and rudimentary forms for measuring public relations activities. However, we contend that the issue is not lack of interest, lack of knowledge, lack of budget, or even a generalized fear of measurement and evaluation. Rather, it is a *perceived lack of usefulness* of these basic content analysis measures that lets them fall into disuse and results in a general lack of measurement and evaluation by the public relations profession.

The Fatal Flaws of Traditional Content Analysis

As comprehensive as these traditional methods of content analysis appear, they still contain significant flaws that severely limit their utility:

- The absence of a basic analytic structure that determines the accuracy of coverage overall and of specific messages included in the content of articles under analysis

- The inability to link analysis to communication goals, objectives, and public relations messages
- A lack of understanding of the communication life cycle

Flaw 1: Not Determining Message Accuracy

The basic accuracy of messages is not generally included among any of the methods of content analysis discussed or considered. Accuracy is a critically important consideration when attempting to link public relations "outputs" to "outcomes" of communications efforts. If a message is erroneous, false, incomplete, or misleading, then the communications efforts are significantly less likely to achieve their objectives (see chapters 1 and 2 for a more detailed discussion on setting objectives).

In order to understand the value of message accuracy in a public relations measurement program, it is important to understand the elements that need to be taken into consideration when conducting this type of analysis. Message accuracy is based on an analysis of four basic elements that become the main units of analysis coded into at least four categories:

- The inclusion of *basic facts*.
  - The inclusion of *misstatements* about these basic facts.
  - The inclusion of *incomplete, deceptive,* or *misleading information* that biases the interpretation of basic facts.
  - The *omission* of basic facts.

Basic Facts. Basic facts are the fundamental information that is central to any communication program. These facts can be such fundamental information as a definition or description of the product or service. They can also include statements, opinions, or points of view that can be supported and documented. Examples of opinions or points of view that can be considered basic facts are statements about *relative value* or *comparative information* that is used to place information in context.

Misstatements. Misstatements are generally understood as errors or incorrect information included in an article or publication. Misstatements typically result from incorrect data but can also include unsubstantiated opinions or points of view from a reporter or inter-viewee who states a falsehood.

Incomplete Information. Incomplete information is a statement, opin-ion, or point of view that selectively includes some information, but excludes other relevant facts. These apparently accurate statements often create misleading impressions or deceptions about a product or service, and while factually accurate, are actually erroneous.

Omissions. Omissions are the absence of key information that *should be included* in a specific article or publication. Not all basic facts can be considered omissions if they are not included in an article or publication. The key to understanding omissions is in the context of the article. The focus or subject matter of the story has to be relevant to the specific omis-sion and the story or article is considered incomplete unless that basic fact is included.

Flaw 2: Not Linking Messages to Communications Objectives

The second challenge involved in conducting effective content analysis is linking communications objectives with the actual message analysis. Typically communications objectives are directly related to the informa-tion needs dictated by a communications life cycle. In public relations, there are two key recipients of these messages. The initial recipient is the media, who, in turn, serve as the conduit for transmitting messages to the intended recipient (i.e., their readers).

Flaw 3: Not Understanding the Communications Life Cycle

All messages have specific goals or objectives. In most cases, these goals or objectives involve having the message recipient take a specific action or indicate intent to take a specific action. These actions can range from making an inquiry about a product or service, to voting for a particular candidate, to developing a favorable image of a brand, company, issue, or organization.

Effective messaging is a process that requires the recipient to go through four stages before a desired action takes place.

These four stages include

1. establishing *awareness* of the brand, the category, or the issue;
2. building *sufficient knowledge and understanding* about the brand, category, or issue in order to make an informed decision;
3. developing a *level of interest in and preference* for the brand, category, or issue, or at least a recognition of its relevance to the message recipient;
4. creating a *change in behavior, intent, or commitment to take a specific action* based on the received messages.

Simply communicating the desire to have a message recipient take an action is unlikely to have the impact a communicator is hoping to achieve. In most cases the analysis fails to account for the stage of the communications life cycle that needs to be addressed. For example, at the initial stage of the communications life cycle, communicators should be measuring the proportion of messages that are strictly designed to develop awareness. At later stages in the life cycle, the analysis needs to shift to determine the proportion of messages that communicate knowledge, interest, or intent to act. (See chapter 2 for a detailed discussion of these factors.)

When this type of analysis is applied, content analysis goes beyond a simple diagnostic of the accuracy of messages, expanding to provide data and evaluation that become an integral part of the strategic communication planning process. Not only can accuracy be measured, but this accuracy can also be directly linked to communication goals that, in turn, can be measured and evaluated among the target audiences for these messages. This analysis is particularly important when each message must be delivered through the media.

The communications life cycle must be understood for both the media as well as from the target audience. In many cases, each can be at a different level of understanding and may have different communication needs. An example is when the media is completely knowledgeable about a product or service, but the target audience has only marginal awareness and little or no understanding. In these instances, the media may make assumptions about the level of knowledge held by the target audience and not report as completely and thoroughly as they should. This can create a gap or omission in an article that needs to be filled. As was pointed out by New York Yankee Hall-of-Fame catcher Yogi Berra, "You've got to be very careful if you don't know where you're going, because you might not get there."

Lessons Learned

The lessons learned from the application of this approach are remarkably simple. In order for content analysis to function as a useful tool, it has to be applied in direct relation to the communication goals and objectives that the content analysis is tracking. While this seems to be a simple and obvious conclusion, the challenge is that these linkages are rarely made, and when they are made, they typically only go partway in meeting the goal or adequately evaluating specific outcomes.

Typically, even when content analysis delves deeply into published materials, these analyses fail to assume that erroneous reporting can be the primary barrier to achieving a program's communication goals. As a result, most content analysis tends to concentrate on the tonality of an article rather than the fundamental correctness of the reporting. This concentration on tonality consequently fails to provide the information that is necessary to implement a corrective strategy with media, which can in turn result in an increase in accurate and appropriately positioned messages.

Content Analysis Case

MetLife and Accuracy of Coverage[9]

Recent award-winning cases involving research on behalf of MetLife are examples where a concentration on the accuracy of coverage has been applied in content analysis. As the results demonstrated, implementing the findings from the initial analysis created measurable improvements in both the quality and accuracy of the coverage as well as the overall volume, resulting in significantly improved media relations.

As these cases show, between 60% and 85% of published articles on the key issues of concern to MetLife included an error in reporting, a misrepresentation of key information or an omission of basic information that should have appeared in the contexts of the articles in question. By concentrating media relations efforts on those reporters and publications where the errors and omissions in reporting occurred, the eventual result was a significant decline in the proportion of articles with either errors or omissions, as well as an overall increase of 45% in the number of articles on the issue at hand. While tonality was not a part of this analysis, the overall effect was that reporting on the issues was much more favorable and more in line with MetLife's media relations goals. The key conclusion drawn from these studies is that shifting the analysis to determining the accuracy of reporting can offer significant benefits that are not available when only tonality is considered. However, this approach has some significant limitations, particularly in comparison with more traditional forms of content analysis.

The primary factors that limit the application of this form of content analysis are the need for in-depth knowledge of the issues in order to determine both erroneous and omitted messages as well as the skill level required to code each article not only for the presence of correct and incorrect messages but also to determine when basic messages should have been included. The latter is particularly critical because it requires that the reader understand the full context of the article in order to code accurately. To date, artificial intelligence systems do not have the capacity to make these determinations. Consequently, highly skilled human coders are required to perform these assessments.

However, human coders need to be rigorously trained and supervised in order to analyze the content both correctly and consistently. In addition, it is highly desirable for these coders to have an intimate knowledge of the issues at hand in order to correctly identify errors in reporting as well as omissions of basic information that should have been included in the article. Without trained and skilled coders, the findings from this research will be highly unreliable and inconsistent.

As a result, the costs for this type of analysis are much higher than for other forms of content analysis. However, the return in a significantly improved quality of media relations as a result of this approach strongly justifies the investment, particularly for the types of products and issues discussed in the case histories on which the article is based. The end result is the overall results demonstrate a substantially higher return than using other methods of content analysis specifically because the analysis concentrates on tying the objectives of the media relations to the content analysis.

A Research Case

Description of the Challenge

Americans often get information on financial planning through the media. This places a very heavy burden and responsibility on editors and reporters to ensure that the information they are sharing with their readers is both accurate and complete. For many middle-market Americans, life insurance should be a significant component of their personal safety nets. Whether or not these consumers were getting the information they need to make informed life insurance purchase decisions—or encouraged by the news media to consider the value of life insurance—prompted MetLife to commission Echo Research to conduct comprehensive research of the consumer media's coverage of life insurance as a product category.

The key challenge for MetLife was identifying how the media reports about life insurance in order to develop a media relations strategy providing critical information to the public and increasing the overall level of accuracy of reporting on this issue.

Strategic Approach

The primary goal of the research was to determine the degree to which correct, incorrect, and only partially correct information was included in news and other stories about life insurance. Going beyond traditional content analysis, an additional goal was the unique effort to determine the extent to which key information about life insurance was omitted or misreported in these articles. The analysis provided a connection between the extent and depth of media coverage on life insurance and the consumers' comprehension of the significance of owning one of the many types of life insurance policies available to them.

The information from this research was used to support broader public relations objectives on life insurance:

- Educating consumers on when to buy life insurance, how much coverage they need, and what type of life insurance best fits their needs

- Educating the media on the benefits of life insurance as an essential life-planning and retirement tool
- Continuing to position MetLife, the largest U.S. life insurer, as a thought leader on life insurance among the national media

Audience Analysis

There were a broad range of audiences for this research, including personal finance reporters, who regularly write about financial issues and protection products, as well as consumers, who rely on the media for their investment and financial planning advice. While this is the general audience for this research, MetLife has a specific interest in those consumers who have the greatest need for reliable and accurate information about life insurance and its benefits—those ages 25 to 44 years old. These consumers are most likely to experience a life event (i.e., getting married, having a child, buying a home) and therefore may have the greatest need for life insurance to protect their families and their assets.

Strategy

Findings from this research served as the basis for a media relations strategy and consumer education program that will communicate the value and benefits of life insurance to key financial planning reporters as well as provide supplemental information to these reporters to ensure their reporting is accurate and complete. This in turn will provide reliable information to the insurance-buying public on these products.

This initiative is driven by the enterprise life insurance strategy team at MetLife, which is composed of product experts, and advertising, brand, eBusiness, marketing, and public relations executives, among others. Included on this team are branding, marketing, advertising, public relations executive, and product managers. These executives view this information as an opportunity to understand what key gaps exist in the American media and how consumer knowledge and behavior are affected.

Research Execution

The research analyzed all articles on life insurance that appeared in the 26 major market daily newspapers with the highest circulation in the United States, leading personal finance publications and websites (e.g., *Money, SmartMoney*, etc.), newswire services, and high-circulation consumer magazines (*Redbook, Self, O, Men's Health*, etc.) from October 1, 2007, through September 30, 2008.

The articles included in the analysis were identified through a keyword search of the Factiva and Nexis databases. The Boolean search string "life insurance" and "purchase" or "purchasing," "buy" or "buying," or "recommend" or "recommending" formed the basis of the search. The search yielded approximately 2,000 articles that met initial search criteria. Based on the initial search, each article was reviewed for content to ensure relevance to the analysis. A total of 237 articles qualified for full review based on this first analysis, yielding 170 articles that were included in the final analysis.

Each article was assessed for overall content and messages. Articles were reviewed and analyzed to determine which messages were correctly reported, misreported, and completely overlooked. The analysis was based on codes organized around three areas: (1) basic facts about life insurance, (2) misstatements about life insurance, and (3) omissions of basic facts about life insurance. Codes were developed by experts at MetLife in consultation with Echo Research and through a review of the articles included in the analysis. Coding was done in the "context" of each article. For example, if the article dealt with product features, codes dealing with cost issues were typically not included in the analysis. This was done to ensure a balanced and fair evaluation of content.

Key Research Findings

The key learning for this study is that life insurance is an essential component of a personal safety net for many Americans, yet too few of its benefits are being conveyed in the media—the central resource that most consumers rely on for reliable information on personal financial planning.

This conclusion is based on the central finding of this research, which identified 19 of 20 articles on life insurance from October 1, 2007, through September 30, 2008, had information gaps that needed to be filled. Overall 94% of all articles published during this period of analysis had at least one error or omission in its reporting on life insurance.

A typical article contained up to three omissions and one misstatement of basic facts about life insurance. Product features and costs were the most common categories where errors and omissions about life insurance occurred. Omissions of basic facts about life insurance were even more prevalent than the inclusion of misstatements. Thirty-two percent of articles contained a misstatement about life insurance. By comparison, 88% of articles omitted a basic fact on this subject. Omitted information is a missed opportunity to provide consumers with essential facts that enable them to make informed decisions on when to buy life insurance, how much coverage they need, and what type of policy best fits their needs.

Surprisingly the most frequent writers on life insurance were not always the most accurate, indicating the need for strong media education programs, even among experienced personal finance writers. Journalists are omitting key information possibly because they either overestimate what the consumer knows about life insurance or they themselves require additional education on the topic. There were very few articles that featured life insurance as a product category. In fact, in 56% of the articles, life insurance received only a passing mention. Only one in five articles mentioning life insurance (20%) went into any significant detail.

The other key finding was that the overall volume of life insurance coverage in 170 articles in a 1-year period was significantly lower than expected. While general mentions of life insurance was higher than other insurance products previously analyzed, overall coverage was much lower than anticipated based on the nature of the product and its universal use. While regional newspapers dominated life insurance coverage, most of the articles originated from wire services or syndicated columns, indicating that life insurance is actually a national story rather than a local story.

Evaluations of Success

As a result of this analysis, MetLife is in the process of developing a proactive media relations strategy that will target personal finance reporters and other consumer media in order to close the key gaps highlighted in the research. These efforts include developing stronger relationships with personal finance reporters at the top-tier media outlets to facilitate more accurate reporting on life insurance. This process has worked successfully in other areas, including income annuities and long-term care insurance—two product areas where MetLife has established itself as the industry thought leader.

PART III

Quantitative Methods for Effective Public Relations Research, Measurement, and Evaluation

Part III introduces the reader to the gathering of information from a *quantitative approach*. Quantitative methods differ from qualitative methods in three major ways. First, quantitative approaches are far less concerned with unique and individual responses; instead, they focus on the gathering of data from larger groups of individuals. Second, many use quantitative methods to generalize to a larger group of individuals through *sampling*. Third, to understand quantitative methods, the researcher must have an understanding of basic *statistical procedures and analyses*. In reality, as will be pointed out later, both qualitative and quantitative methods are required in public relations research—the professional, unlike his or her marketing counterparts, must understand the unique perceptions of the opinion leaders who are targeted to serve as third-party endorsers of the messages being sent out by a campaign. In this way qualitative and quantitative methods are complementary to each other.

This section begins by examining the major quantitative method employed in public relations—the *survey* (chapter 7). At the end of that chapter is an introduction to experimental methodology, through which precampaign testing and academic research focusing on questions of definition and fact are found. Chapter 8 examines *statistical analysis*, which is the cornerstone of quantitative analysis and evaluation. It then builds on this foundation for chapter 9, which discusses *sampling*. Sampling allows the researcher to obtain smaller samples that are representative of the larger population or public under study.

CHAPTER 7

Survey Methodology

As noted earlier, research can take many forms. It may focus on unique and individual responses that provide rich information about a problem or project, or it may focus on an understanding of how large groups of individuals perceive a problem or a project. This type of research is called *quantitative research*. When the researcher asks questions about larger groups of individuals from a quantitative approach, that researcher is seeking *normative data*. Normative data provide information on larger groups that then can be further subdivided by nominal or ordinal data (see chapter 3) and compared, or they can be compared against data gathered by others from similar groups.

The primary method employed in public relations to gather such data is *survey methodology*. This chapter introduces the concept of a survey and its component parts. At the end of the chapter, a special form of survey methodology is examined, one that is often used in academia and sometimes in marketing and advertising, but seldom in public relations—the *experiment*. The major difference between a survey and an experiment is control of the respondent. In a survey, the researcher is seeking information without setting restrictive conditions. The respondent can be at home, on the telephone, with the television on and the survey can still be conducted. In an experiment, that same respondent is in the same environment as all other respondents, which controls any intervening variables—things that may change responses or contaminate the respondents perceptions of what is being studied.

The Survey as Quantitative Methodology

The Dictionary of Public Relations Measurement and Research defines a quantitative methodology as one that "usually refers to studies that are highly objective and projectable, using closed-ended, forced-choice questionnaires."[1] Further, it states that quantitative research "relies heavily on statistics and numerical measures."[2] Survey methodology is defined as "a formal research methodology that seeks to gather data and analyze a population's or sample's attitudes, beliefs, and opinions"[3] Such a survey is appropriate when the researcher needs to better understand how a large group of individuals perceives some attitude object—whether it is an organization, an individual, or a product.

Qualifying Evaluation of Survey Data

Before turning to the conducting of a survey, it is important to note three things that qualify how survey data are evaluated. First, how the data have been gathered qualifies what can be done with them. This is the qualifier of *sampling*, covered later in this chapter and in more detail in chapter 9. Second, how responses are assessed qualifies how the data can be evaluated. This is the qualifier of *causality*, which states that what individuals perceive is a function of some particular public relations strategy conducted prior to respondent contact. Third, the type of questions being asked qualifies how the data can be assessed and evaluated. This is the qualifier of *questionnaire construction*. All three of these qualifiers must be taken into account when evaluating the data gathered by a survey.

Polls Versus Surveys

Polls and surveys are both quantitative approaches to gathering data on large groups of individuals. The primary differences between the two are simple. *Polls*, "a form of survey research that focuses more on immediate behavior than attitudes,"[4] yield short, *behaviorally driven*, quantitatively gathered data.[5] They seek to quickly assess the intended actions or immediate short-term perceptions of a sample or population. Surveys, on the other hand, seek to understand why groups hold particular opinions through an analysis of their attitudes, beliefs, and values on a particular topic. The survey is therefore much longer and requires more secondary research in writing the survey questionnaire. Both have places as quantitative tools in the public relations professional's research toolkit.

Designing a Survey or Poll

Although it may be tempting to just sit down and write a survey or poll questionnaire, there are five considerations the researcher must address. These considerations, which come from secondary research, are, in order, (1) What is known about the population under study and the concepts or behaviors or attitudes being assessed? (2) What is being studied: potential or actual behavior or attitudes, beliefs, and values? (3) What is the best way to contact potential respondents? (4) Given the research question and communication plan objectives, how many times are respondents contacted? (5) What sort of sampling, if any, is to be conducted?

1. The "Frame"

Unless the researcher has the resources to contact each and every respondent available, some sort of parameters need to be placed on who will be studied. Basically there is a *universe* of people that can be sampled, but some of these are not of interest and can be excluded for both that reason and economics. That leaves the researcher with a public of interest within what now might be considered a *population*. Populations, however, are quite large and may need to be broken down further into an audience composed of *demographics*. It is when the researcher has determined just exactly who will be contacted that she has defined the *frame* of her survey or poll. A survey frame, later to be refined as a *sampling frame*, might be interested in active voters of either sex of middle-class families who have at least three credit cards. Hence the survey would not be interested in people who have not voted in a specified time period or who are not registered voters or who are part of the upper or lower economic classes, but would include both males and females. The survey frame sets the conditions of who will be contacted and, with sufficient secondary research, can be compared against known data—typically U.S. census data—for estimates of sample reliability and validity.

2. Survey Type

The researcher must then consider what type of survey to conduct. Is this a topic that is more behaviorally oriented and does not require a more in-depth understanding of motivations or information? If so, then the researcher will conduct a poll—a short set of questions that can be answered quickly, usually on a "yes" or "no" basis. For instance, for people known to reside in an upper-income neighborhood based on U.S. census data, the poll may ask a couple of questions—"Are you planning on voting in the next bond election?" followed by "Will you support the bond proposal?" Because the researcher already knows a lot about the neighborhood from the census data, and if a telephone contact, be fairly certain about the respondent's sex, not much more is needed.

If the researcher is interested in how much information the respondent has seen about a product, where that information was observed, and what the respondent thinks and feels about the product, then a survey will be required. Surveys are much longer and require more thought. Hence it is more costly to administer a survey and it takes longer to analyze the data, but a survey will yield considerably more information on respondents.

3. Contacting Respondents

There are numerous ways to contact respondents, each with advantages and disadvantages. Traditional approaches include person-to-person, mail, and telephone. Contemporary approaches use social media, computer networks, and automated calling. Approaches to contacting respondents—and the reactions of respondents to being contacted—have changed dramatically in the last 30 to 40 years. At one time, it was an honor to be contacted for your opinion on a product, political party, company, or individual, and being contacted was a rare occurrence. Today, potential respondents are being bombarded with requests, often not from research firms, but from marketing agencies trying to sell a product under the guise of a survey or poll. Respondents now filter requests and often simply refuse to respond to survey or poll requests.

Regardless of the contact approach, all surveys and polls should report three things: (1) how the respondents were selected, (2) how the

respondents were contacted, and (3) how many respondents participated, including the percentage of completed surveys compared against
attempts at contact. A "good" response rate varies by the approach, but in
general response rates have dropped significantly over the last 20 years.[6]
Sometimes an incentive is offered to increase response rates. For instance,
a coupon for a discount on a product or an advance copy of the results or
report may be offered for completion. When this is done, the researcher
must follow through with the promised action.

Traditional Contact Approaches

Perhaps the oldest form of contact is the *person-to-person* approach. Here,
individual interviewers are sent out to conduct survey interviews face to
face with respondents. These are expensive when you take into consideration the costs of transportation and duplication of materials, but the
advantage is that the *selected* respondent, if available, is identified as the
correct respondent. A downside of this approach is that interviewers often
have to go to areas that may not be safe. The typical person-to-person
approach aims to survey slightly more than 400 individuals. Why 400?
This is the magic number that survey researchers and pollsters use to
ensure that their sample represents 95% of who their intended sample
and that respondents will error in their responses no more than 5% of
the time. Because the researcher is targeting specific individuals through
a process where he basically knows who and where the respondents live, a
60% response rate for completed surveys is considered "good."[7]

A variation of the person-to-person contact approach is the *intercept*.
As the label implies, contact is made by intercepting people in a particular location. This is a variation of the "man on the street" intercept. In
the intercept approach, respondents are selected because of their location,
and this is reported in the write-up of the results. Typically these interviews are conducted in shopping malls. The mall intercept allows the
researcher to target specific respondents, and can be used when research-
ing responses or reactions to particular products. As will be seen later, it is
a way to bring an experiment to the "field."[8]

Almost all of us have been approached to participate in a *telephone survey* at one time or another. The telephone approach has several advantages

over other contact methods. First, calls can be targeted to specific individuals or groups from an identified list, giving us a pretty good idea of who the respondent is and basic census data can be obtained for the telephone exchange and number. Second, the number of call attempts and completed calls for each number provides the researcher with easily computed response rates. Third, if a respondent is not available, a systematic method can be used to choose another respondent. Fourth, telephone calls can be made to areas where it might be dangerous for an interviewer to go or may be so far from the researcher that it is impossible to contact the individual. Finally, telephone surveys can be conducted fairly quickly.

The disadvantages? First, telephone surveying is relatively expensive, as the researcher will have to either invest in a bank of telephones or rent a phone bank from a provider. Second, calling times are generally restricted. No one likes having their dinner interrupted, so the researcher needs to understand local time zones and try to call between dinner and bedtime, usually 7:00 p.m. to no later than 11:00 p.m. Third, the type of questions that can be asked is limited. Although open-ended questions may be necessary, they are hard to get respondents to complete, and the interviewer must write exactly what the respondent said (this is often done by having the interviewer record all answers on a computer). Finally, language can be a problem. If a respondent does not speak English, for instance, the interviewer cannot translate the survey or questions, or provide guidance as to what a particular word or phrase means. Good telephone response rates used to be in the 50% to 60% range. However, with all the filtering equipment now available (including caller ID, answering machines being used to screen calls, and cell phones), an excellent response rate is around 30%.

Finally, there is the *mail* approach. In this approach respondents are contacted through the mail, typically the U.S. Postal Service, and asked to complete a paper-and-pencil questionnaire and return it to the researcher. Advantages of the mail survey include respondents being able to see the questionnaire, complete open-ended questions, and provide the researcher with different opinion, attitude, or belief measures (see chapter 3). For instance, while a telephone survey is limited to category-centered measures, such as the Likert scale, a mail survey can use semantic differential scales or visual scales. The disadvantages of the mail survey include cost (duplicating, stuffing, postage), not knowing exactly who completed the questionnaire, and problems with mailing lists and out-dated addresses. A good response rate used to be in the 60% range, but today a good response rate is in the 20% range. According to one survey researcher, however, employing a five-step process can still yield response rates in the 60% range, but the costs associated with this method are rather high.[9]

Contemporary Contact Approaches

Contemporary contact approaches employ most of the "bells and whistles" available with modern communications. However, some of these approaches have produced a harsh backlash for people engaged in honest survey research and polling. The worst offenders are companies that utilize *computer-generated calls* with computerized responses—no actual human is "interviewing" respondents. Most of us have received a computer-generated survey. Typically it begins with a short time delay and then a voice. They typically ask the respondent to provide responses by selecting a particular number on the phone keypad or replying with a "yes" or "no" response.

Perhaps the biggest push lately has come in the area of *Internet surveys*. Internet surveys combine the advantages of mail surveys with the speed of telephone surveys. The researcher employs a web-based survey program (e.g., SurveyMonkey, Zoomerang, mrInterview) and creates a questionnaire, links it to a file of e-mail addresses, and sends it out. Internet surveys are fast, but response rates are generally low; indeed, many marketing survey companies have sprung up that actively seek "panels" of people who are paid or offered some form of inducement to "evaluate" products. Specialized samples may yield higher survey responses, but general population responses are lower than might expected with traditional contact methods. A disadvantage of Internet surveys is a problem with anonymity and confidentiality as e-mail addresses are identified in the returned surveys. This can be addressed by stripping all e-mail addresses prior to reviewing the responses. An advantage of Internet surveys using web survey programs is that basic statistical analysis is provided as part of the package (see chapter 8 for more on statistical analysis). Internet-based surveys have an inherent bias due to the fact that only those who are Internet users and who have registered are invited to participate.

Problems with Internet surveys have led to a *social network approach*. Instead of asking potential respondents to complete a survey sent to them (called the *opt-out* approach), a plea is made for interested respondents to go to a website and participate in the survey (called the *opt-in* approach). As will be briefly discussed a little later in this chapter and in more detail in chapter 9, this approach does not allow the researcher to generalize her findings to the larger population.

4. Data Gathering Approaches

Once the survey contact approach has been decided, the next question is what type of survey or poll will be employed. There are two basic survey designs: cross-sectional and longitudinal. The difference between them deals, first, with how many times contact is made and, second, who is contacted if the particular study requires study over time.

Cross-Sectional Design

Surveys and polls employing a *cross-sectional design* only run the survey once and for a specified period of time. The cross-sectional survey or poll is probably the most used design in all of survey research. As the name suggests, it seeks to report on a specific cross section of a population at a specific time.

The *longitudinal design*, as the label implies, is a study that is done over time, usually employing the same questionnaire over that time period. (Using different questionnaires over time is equivalent to comparing apples to oranges.) The longitudinal survey can be further broken into three types: trend, panel, and cohort. The *trend* survey employs *different* respondent samples from the *same* population over time. That is, the survey is administered over a time period multiple times but with different samples from the same population. The *panel* survey employs the *same* respondents from the population over time. It takes a relatively large sample of respondents (because respondents will drop out—fail to continue to participate for any of a number of reasons) and asks them to complete the survey questionnaire over a specified period of time. The *cohort-trend* survey employs *different* respondents from the population over time, but respondents are selected from a *subpopulation* of interest that is referred to as its "constant."[10] The subpopulation may be a sample of first-time purchasers of a product taken yearly, or it could be from an organization's retirees yearly.

5. Sampling

Sampling refers to the actual selection of respondents for a survey or poll. Sampling will be covered in detail in chapter 9, but a quick overview should put survey planning into perspective. There are three basic ways to select respondents. First, you can contact each and every respondent in your population, which is a *census* of that population. The key is that you cannot miss one respondent. Second, you can conduct a *random* or *probability sample* of the population. A random sample means that you are selecting respondents through a process whereby *each and every respondent has an equal chance of being chosen to participate in the* survey. A random sample allows the researcher to draw inferences from the sample and generalize them to the larger population within specified degrees of sampling and measurement error. Finally, you can conduct a *nonprobability* sample. A nonprobability sample draws from respondents who are available to the researcher, and inferences can only be made to those who completed the survey.

Summary

Conducting a survey or poll should be approached with a thorough understanding of why the research is being conducted and for whom. Often surveys generate results requiring more research of a qualitative nature be conducted. Sometimes qualitative methods are used to prepare for survey research. Clearly the qualitative and quantitative methodologies should be approached as complimentary to each other. When both qualitative and quantitative methods are used, the research is said to be "triangulated."[11] We turn next to the actual writing of a survey instrument—the questionnaire.

Questionnaire Construction

Creating a poll questionnaire is fairly straightforward, while creating a survey questionnaire is much more difficult. The poll questionnaire is short, to the point, and focused on intended or actual behavior; thus "yes" and "no" questions are about all that are required. The survey questionnaire, however, seeks to assess and evaluate respondents' attitudes, beliefs, and values toward some expected behavior in the future. As such, it is much longer on average and requires considerable thought. However, the questionnaire can be approached from its four main sections—introduction, body of questions, demographics, and closing. Before actually beginning to write a questionnaire, however, the way it will be transmitted to respondents must be considered, as this will change how the questions are stated and respondents will answer.

Introduction

It would seem intuitive that a questionnaire should begin with an introduction, but this is not always the case. There is a difference between an introduction and directions on how to complete the questionnaire. A survey or poll questionnaire should begin with a short introduction that does three things. First, it introduces the respondent to the sponsor and whatever research organization might be conducting the survey. This serves to establish the credibility of the project. Second, it should assure respondents that their responses will be kept anonymous and confidential. Anonymity and confidentiality are especially important in surveys where respondents are asked questions about their attitudes and beliefs. Finally, it affords a bit of interpersonal communication. If telephone or person-to-person contact is employed, it should also allow the respondent to refuse to participate.[12] The telephone or person-to-person introduction is a script that is read by the interviewer, while the other contact approaches are read by the respondent. Regardless, the introduction should be short and to the point.

For example,

> The survey you are being asked to complete is being conducted for X company by ABC Survey Research. We are engaged in a study assessing the public's perception of product Z. The survey will take approximately XX minutes and requires that you simply respond by indicating the most appropriate responses. There are no right or wrong responses, only your perspective on them. You will remain anonymous at all times and all responses will be held in strictest confidence. Please take the XX minutes to complete the survey and return it to us by . . .

An adaptation of this introduction for verbal transmission might begin with, "Hi, my name is _____, and I'm conducting a survey for X Company . . ."

Body

The questionnaire body contains the meat of the survey. Usually the questionnaire begins with general questions and statements and then moves to more specific questions and responses. All questionnaires should use transitions such as "Next" or "Please answer the following questions by . . ." between sections. In a telephone or person-to-person survey the transitions, called "sign posts," keep the respondent's interest up and simultaneously maintain a steady rate of completion. A special type of body question is the *filter question*. A filter question moves respondents from one part of the body to another, including moving the respondent to the closing section. For instance, if the study is only concerned with respondents who regularly read newspapers (defined by the study's purpose), a filter question might be "Are you a regular newspaper reader? Yes or No?" If no, the respondent is sent, or "skipped," to the closing section in a written survey or the interviewer would move immediately to the closing section. A filter question can serve as a filter to a previous filter question: "Do you read a newspaper at least five times a week? Yes or No?" with the same decisions being made depending on the response.

How the questionnaire's questions and statements are laid out depends on the contact method employed. For instance, a Likert-type statement (see chapter 3) in a questionnaire might be written as

> Please respond to the following statements as to whether you Strongly Agree (SA), Agree (A), Neither Agree Nor Disagree (N), Disagree (D), or Strongly Disagree with each.
> I think that abortion is a woman's choice
>   SA   A   N   D   SD
> Third trimester abortions should be legal
>   SA   A   N   D   SD

In a written format, the respondent sees the instructions, the statements, and that the responses are equal appearing. The verbal format, however, requires that the instructions and statements be read exactly *as is* and the response categories *stated for each and every statement*. In the verbal format, respondents quickly pick up the responses and will respond before the interviewer finishes the categories.

Demographics

All surveys or polls have a section that seeks to better understand who is responding to the study. This is the *demographic section,* which includes not only *demographic data,* such as sex, age, income, education, and so forth, but can include *psychographic data* (interests, hobbies, likes and dislikes) and *netgraphic data* (social media used, social networks belonged to). Respondents are often unwilling to provide demographic data, so most surveys put the demographic section at the end of the questionnaire. The exception is when a demographic is used as a filter question and it must be asked early, such as in voting studies or studies where use or knowledge of a product is required. Many surveys use a demographic filter question seeking to avoid respondents who have backgrounds in public relations, marketing, and advertising or those who work for the company or client for whom the survey is being conducted. Please note that these questions can be quite sensitive and caution needs exercised in their wording. These questions typically concern age ("How old are you?" "In what year were you born?"), education ("What is the highest educational level completed?" usually asked in the form of an ordinal list beginning with elementary school through graduate school), and household or personal income (usually an ordinal list tied to known income demographics).

Closing

Finally, the closing section ends the survey. This section serves several purposes. First, it takes the time or space to thank the respondent for his or her time. Second, it provides information that the respondent can use to follow-up on participation or provides contact information on how to get in touch with the survey team. Third, it is often used when some promise is made regarding an inducement for participation and tells respondents how to receive the inducement and assuring anonymity and confidentiality. A sample closing statement might be the following:

> Thank you very much for completing this survey. Your responses will help us better understand X. If you would like more information or have any questions regarding the survey, please contact XX at XXX. [Should you wish to claim your coupon for X, please include your contact information here: _____. We will not include this information in the study and your responses will remain anonymous and confidential.]

(The material in brackets would be if an incentive were used to increase response rates.)

The Experiment as a Special Case

Earlier in this chapter we noted that a survey can also be used as part of an experiment. An *experiment* is a research project that attempts to carefully control any outside influence on the results. When we think of an experiment, we think of the traditional *laboratory experiment*.[13] Although laboratory experiments are conducted in public relations, they are conducted mostly by academics testing relationships between variables. Because they are highly controlled, they cannot be generalized beyond their carefully controlled conditions, but they do provide evidence of *causal relationships*.

A causal relationship states that if one thing happens, another happens as a result. To establish causation three things must occur:

- First, *it must be established beyond doubt that a change in one thing (variable) causes a change in another thing (variable)*.
- Second, it must be established whether the variable associated with causing the change actually precedes the change in the second variable; that is, *the effect actually follows the cause*.
- Third, *it must be shown beyond doubt that no other variables influenced the causal relationship*.

Only a carefully controlled experimental study can do this. An experimental study interviews a random group of people ("subjects" or "participants") who are randomly assigned to "conditions" in which certain variables are manipulated. An experimental study also includes a "control group," which receives no manipulation or exposure to the variables that are expected to create a causal effect.[14]

What makes the survey qualify as a special experimental case? There are four specific conditions that have to be met:

1. Randomly selecting participants
2. Screening participants for specific qualities that meet the conditions set forth by the research
3. Randomly assigning some to "experimental conditions" where they are manipulated (they are exposed to the experimental stimulus) and respond to the questionnaire
4. Randomly assigning some to "control conditions" where they receive no manipulation (they only complete the questionnaire)

This is exactly what the public relations "multiplier effect" studies did, but they went further.[15] To ensure that the results were not biased due to where people lived, the study was conducted at six malls across the United States. In one study, 350 shoppers who were daily newspaper readers participated; in the second study, more than 600 shoppers who read daily newspapers and shopped those same malls participated. The results failed to find the "multiplier effect" for public relations over advertising, but did provide data that the public relations efforts increased product knowledge and could be correlated to participant feelings toward the product.

Most public relations professionals will not engage in experimentation, but a true understanding of experimental studies published by academics and others is invaluable when conducting secondary research that will lead to qualitative or quantitative research. Understanding what variables should cause an effect provides a strategic advantage in developing public relations programs and campaigns.

Case Study: Broward County Public Schools Community Involvement Department Survey

In 2003 the Community Involvement Department of the Broward County Public Schools determined that they needed to establish a baseline of knowledge, awareness, and perceptions of its community involvement program by county school administrators and teachers. The department's programs involved a number of initiatives that brought community leaders and parents into the classroom. In particular, they wished to ascertain the baseline on what were then schools that had received "Five Star" ratings of excellence and had participated in the department's community involvement programs.

Background

The Broward County Public School's Community Involvement Department ran a number of programs they thought enhanced student and teacher educational experiences. While the department had in place extensive mentor, parent, community partner, and volunteer programs, no systematic assessment of teaching and administrative awareness, knowledge, and attitudes regarding the program had been undertaken. It was hoped that research would accomplish two objectives. First, it would provide a baseline of awareness, knowledge, and attitudes toward the department's programs from top-ranked, Five Star schools. Second, the research would serve to validate the department's vision and mission as related to the Broward County Public School's vision and mission.

Secondary Research

The department brought in a survey researcher to work with them on the research project. Prior to the first meeting, he was sent materials relevant to the project, including Broward County Public Schools mission and vision background information and data, summaries of the department's own discussions of their mission and vision, and other relevant information. During a face-to-face discussion study parameters were established and a decision was made to target "successful" schools as best practice examples, with the target audiences split between Five Star elementary, middle school, and high school teachers and administrators.

Sample

The sample consisted of administrators and teachers from 34 Five Star schools (14 elementary, 9 middle, and 11 high schools) active in the department's community involvement programs. The decision to sample only Five Star schools sought to gather data from "best practice" schools. The sample was split into administrators (a census of all 110 administrators) and teachers (400 were randomly selected across the three school levels from a listing of all teachers' home addresses at the 34 schools). The survey employed a mail format and a modified Dillman five-step process[16] was followed. Warning cards were sent to all respondents in late May, 1 week prior to sending out the questionnaire packet. Two weeks after that a reminder card was sent, and a new packet was sent 2 weeks after the reminder. A final reminder card was sent to all respondents 2 weeks after that. The study was conducted during the summer of 2003. Because the survey was conducted over the summer months, and knowing there would be address errors due to movement and reassignments, it was decided that any selected respondent whose initial card was returned by the post office would be replaced by a simple random selection of a new respondent; thus, 80 respondents were dropped from the sample due to address errors and 80 replacements were added using a random-number generator. Ten administrator cards were returned as "undeliverable," so the sample consisted of 100 of 110 possible administrators.

Questionnaire Development

The survey sought to assess teacher and administrator awareness, knowledge, and attitudes toward the department's mentor, parent, partner, and volunteer programs and the extent to which respondents believed that five special audiences (school board, teachers, parents, students, and community partners) identified with 15 specific values the department felt served to enhance their mission in regard to the larger school board mission. The questionnaire began with an introductory paragraph describing the project, how respondents were selected, and a guarantee of anonymity and confidentiality, and ended with a short paragraph of thanks for participating. The working elements were broken into five sections, beginning with individual demographic data dealing with school-related questions (e.g., what grade was taught, how many years at the current school) and four personal questions (highest degree earned, year born for age calculations [i.e., "In what year were you born? 19__"], sex, and race [White, Black, Hispanic, Asian, or Other, with space for input]). Because all respondents were involved in some way with the community involvement programs, which were being assessed, demographic data were collected first, unlike many surveys where the data are obtained last. The second section addressed their participation in the community involvement program. The third section asked about respondent perceptions of the community involvement program. The fourth section addressed community involvement across the five special audiences. The fifth section asked open-ended questions.

Because there were two subsamples, slightly different questionnaires were created for teachers and administrators. The teacher questionnaire was phrased in the first person (e.g., "I believe," "I have," "your"), while the administrator questionnaire was phrased toward the school as well as the respondent (e.g., "My school," "My faculty," and "I have"). The demographic data questions for administrators only differed from the teachers in terms of duties (administering versus teaching; title versus grade level taught). The second section's instructions differed in terms of orientation; administrators were asked to provide information regarding "your school's Community Involvement Division programs and your relationship with it," while teachers were instructed to provide information regarding "programs you indicated participating in above program [from the demographic section] and your relationship with them."

The third section contained a large number of 5-point Likert-type statements using a "strongly agree" to "strongly disagree" continuum written to assess the department's community involvement strategies and priorities. Again, two different sets of questions were created, one for teachers that employed 45 statements from the teacher's perspective (e.g., "I visit") and included statements of parent input, staff input, resource availability, community input, their school improvement plan, and student input; in addition, several statements assessed the perceptions of school administrators. The administrator section employed 40 statements (e.g., "My faculty visit") at the individual school level, but did not seek administrative data.

The fourth section provided respondents with a matrix of the department's 15 core values identified across the five selected audiences. Respondents were asked to check which core values they felt each specific audience identified with (school board; administrators focused on teachers, while teachers focused on their school; parents; students; and community partners). The resultant matrix provided data about departmental values that could be broken by audience or by value.

Finally, a number of open-ended questions were asked to help better understand respondents' perceptions of the department. Teachers and administrators were asked how other teachers and administrators or friends would describe the community involvement program, what recommendations they had that might make the community involvement program better, and anything that was positive or negative that the department should know about.

Results

By the end of the summer, 45 administrators and 132 teachers, representing all three school levels, had returned questionnaires, yielding a total response rate of 35.4% (45% administrator; 33% teacher). The sample size was considered acceptable due to moves and vacations during the summer months when teachers were not teaching.

The results were instructive and the department was received data that helped them to better understand how their programs were being received, where there might be problems, and how the department's values were identified across key audiences.

Summary

The survey established a baseline against which future surveys dealing with information flow, perceptions and attitudes, and identification with the Community Involvement Department could be compared for progress in meeting departmental goals and objectives. It also pointed out areas of commonality between administrators and teachers, as well a need for better communication flow from the department to the administrator to the teacher.

Best Practices

What makes a best practice survey? First, the study objectives clearly reflect the overall communication program goals and objectives. Second, secondary research is conducted that links what is known regarding the survey object of study to what the researcher needs to know. If the survey is attempting to determine behavioral indicators, then a poll may be most appropriate; if it attempts to better understand attitudes, beliefs, or values, a survey may be most appropriate. Third, sampling decisions are made based on what is known about the population, then a sampling frame is established. Fourth, the questionnaire is designed, written, and checked to ensure that it flows well. This requires several decisions regarding transitions, mainly a function of how the survey is to be conducted—mail, telephone, Internet, person-to-person all require slight modifications in terms of instructions and transitional statements. Fifth, the sample design is determined and the survey type selected. Finally, if time allows, a pretest with a sample from a larger population is conducted. Best practice survey research is not something done on the spur of the moment. As with other methods, it should be planned and executed according to a plan that is closely tied to the larger communication and business plan.

Summary

Survey research provides a way to gather data from a large and diverse population. If conducted through random selection, it allows a researcher to generalize the results within degrees of sampling and measurement error to the larger population. If conducted as a nonprobability sample, the researcher must confine drawing conclusions and summarizing findings to the sample drawn. Regardless, the survey is a popular quantitative method employed in public relations as a way to gather data that will lead to a better understanding of how the targeted sample or population perceive the object under study.

CHAPTER 8

Statistical Analysis

Quantitative research, by its very nature, is closely associated with numbers and coming to conclusions based on those numbers. When researchers use a quantitative method they take numerical data and interpret them through *statistical reasoning*. Statistical reasoning can be approached in two ways, depending on the nature of the research and its uses. The first way is to use the numerical data to simply *describe* variables in the study. This is called *descriptive statistical reasoning*. Often surveys will report what was found through the research in terms that simply describe how many respondents answered statements or as levels of a particular variable, such as sex (48 females or 48% of the sample as compared to 52 males or 52% of the sample felt the product was a good buy for its price). The statistics simply describe the results. The second way is to use the numerical data to *infer* differences between levels of a variable. This is called *inferential statistical reasoning*. Here the numerical data are used to establish the *probability* that groups of people are truly different. In the preceding example, for instance, is 48 actually smaller than 52? Or is there no real difference between female and male perceptions on that product? Inferential statistical reasoning provides a way to test—to infer—for differences.

This chapter will cover both descriptive and inferential statistical reasoning from a practical perspective. It will not require the understanding of complex statistical formulas, but instead will demonstrate how numerical data can be used to present findings and then interpret those findings in terms of their probability of differences. As such, there is very little mathematics involved. Indeed, statistical analysis, especially today with computerized statistical packages such as IBM® SPSS® Statistics,[1] is more about understanding how to read a map and what that map represents. The analogy to a map is appropriate in that statistics provide the directions from which inferences can be made about numerical data, but each "map" is slightly different, just as maps used to travel differ between geographical and political representations of the same territory. Before we turn to descriptive statistical reasoning, a quick review of "data" and how we define and label data is necessary.

Describing Data

In chapter 3 we noted that data can take many different forms. For statistical purposes, however, data are associated with numbers and "numerical thinking." Because of this, people often assume that data—numbers— have some direct meaning. From the outset, let us agree that *numbers have no meaning in and of themselves, but meaning is interjected into them by people collecting, analyzing, and reporting those numbers.* That is, a number is simply an indicator—an often imprecise indicator—that provides us with the ability to make comparisons. In chapter 3, numbers were defined by the type of data being collected or observed. We noted that there were two major types of data—categorical and continuous—and within each type there were two subclasses.

Categorical and Continuous Data

When employing statistical reasoning, especially when we are attempting to infer differences from data, how the data are initially defined becomes important. As covered in detail in chapter 3, categorical analyses can result from either nominal or ordinal data—which in the former simply differentiates levels of an object or variable and in the latter proposes an ordering effect for levels of the object or variable. For instance, nominal data for sex would be defined as female or male, with each being equated equally and simply a way to distinguish the levels. However, for ordinal data, such as socioeconomic status, the variables lower class, middle class, and upper class are not only different but also ordered in terms of lowest to highest status. Note, too, that categorical data are *always* categorical data, even when analyses may *appear* to be continuous (e.g., percentages). Continuous analyses resulting from interval (e.g., age) or ratio (e.g., monetary data such as dollars or pounds sterling) data put the data on a range or continuum. As noted in chapter 3, continuous data can be reduced to categorical data, but categorical data cannot be modified to become continuous data.

The first step in statistical reasoning is to understand how the data were defined before being collected. This provides the basic information required to determine which statistic is most appropriate to report and interpret. The second step is to actually compute the statistic by "running" the data either by hand or via a computer.

Using Computer Programs to Calculate Statistics

The computer has made all of us statisticians. This is not necessarily a good thing. A computer can compute any statistic asked for, whether or not it is the appropriate statistic for the data or problem. Further, new statistical packages often "help" in deciding what statistic should be run. The computer is actually only as smart as the user, so understanding what statistic to run should come from the research objectives, which of course reflect the larger public relations and business objectives. Some statistical packages have evolved into large programs that not only run the statistics requested but also have fairly good graphing programs. Other computer programs simply run the statistics requested and provide output for analysis. There are a large number of computerized *statistical* packages available, including IBM® SPSS® Statistics and SAS (large, comprehensive programs) and Minitab and Statistics With Finesse (smaller, less comprehensive programs).[2] In addition, there are analytical packages that combine both the analytics, such as content analysis, and basic statistical analyses. These programs include survey packages such as Zoomerang and SurveyMonkey, as well as dedicated statistical analysis programs such as Mentor and statistical add-on programs that can be used in conjunction with Microsoft Office applications like Excel. Analyse-it and SPC XL are two of the most commonly used of these add-on programs.

The computer also allows researchers to provide clients with sophisticated visual presentations of the data. These *dashboards* or *scorecards* are simply descriptive statistics that are updated at intervals ranging from daily to monthly to quarterly. Figures 8.1 and 8.2 present two such visual representations of a number of variables representing verbal descriptions, categorical data, and continuous data. We will refer back to these when discussing visualizing descriptive data.

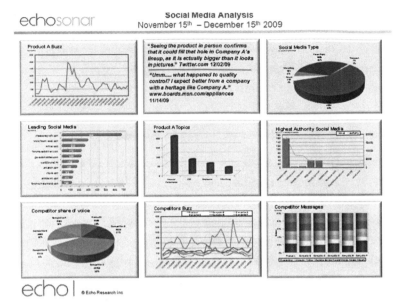

Figure 8.1. Sample scorecard with pie, column, and bar charts.
Used with permission of Echo Research.

Descriptive Statistical Reasoning

Descriptive statistics, as noted earlier, simply describe or summarize the data. All quantitative research and some qualitative research describe data. The simplest level of description is to summarize the data for one variable, or to conduct a *univariate descriptive analysis*. More complex analyses summarize the data for two or more variables, or conduct *bivariate* or *multivariate descriptive analyses*. Bivariate and multivariate analyses summarize the data by each variable's levels, such as sex (male or female) and socioeconomic status (lower, middle, and upper):

	Lower Class	Middle Class	Upper Class
Female			
Male			

© Echo Research

Company A   U.S. Media Analysis Report
- November 15th – December 31st, 2009

Key Performance Indicators
Highlights

	Company A
Period:	November 15 – December 28, 2009
Volume:	55
% Favorable:	63.6
% Unfavorable:	7.3
% Neutral:	29.1
Imps (millions):	20.4
Rating:	55.5 (see final page for explanation)

Competitor Comparison: Company A
by volume, favorability & rating

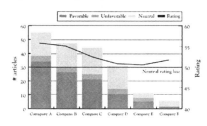

SWOT ANALYSIS: Company A
by volume & rating

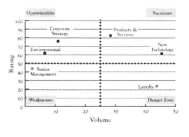

Insight & Recommendations

- **RESEARCH BACKGROUND:** This report measured and evaluated competitive mentions of the Company A across traditional and social media during the period November 15th to December 28th 2009. Relevant news items were monitored daily across several media types including print, online, social media (blogs, forums, comments, etc.) and broadcast (TV and radio) sources. Competitors included the Company B, Company C, Company D, Company E, Company F, Company G and Company H. See attached PDF for full explanation of Echo Research's research method.

- **COMPETITIVE PERFORMANCE:** Company A was successful based on its rating, competitive positioning and mentions of the Convention Center Show. Benefitting from its introduction, Company A led the segment for overall volume, favorable volume and rating. Company B was second and well positioned on technology and fuel efficiency. Company C was third and praised for its reputation as a safe, reliable product. The other competitors generated minimal mentions and few key messages.

- **MEDIA OVERVIEW:** Traditional media, mainly regional newspapers, produced Company A's best mix of volume and rating. Social media was less successful as few sites of high authority contained online conversations about Company A (authority is based on links to other sites and re-posting of content).

- **KEY MESSAGES & PR-DRIVEN COVERAGE:** Company A was well-positioned as a fuel efficient product leading the way for the new Company A. Of concern: fuel efficiency overshadowed other key messages such as design, safety and performance. PR-driven mentions were a major factor behind Company A's strong rating. Nearly 65% of all Company A, coverage either featured press material, the Convention Center Show coverage or quotes from corporate or division spokespeople. Competitively, the only product with notable PR-driven coverage was from Company B.

- **OVERALL RECOMMENDATION:** Get the word out that Company A's product is more than just a fuel efficient product, especially given its well-established competition. The SWOT analysis to the left illustrates how Company A's corporate situation can impact the product. The product will benefit from keeping corporate mentions to a minimum. With social media, be more strategic and engaged through key spokespeople – the product has been favorably mentioned, but sites with high authority lack any real conversation or buzz between influencers / consumers and Company A.

Figure 8.2. Scorecard with summarized bivariate tables and stacked column and bar charts.

Used with permission of Echo Research.

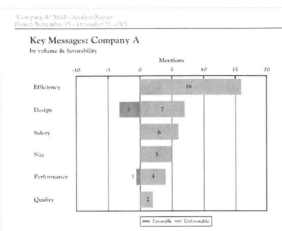

Key Messages: Company A
by volume & favorability

The strength of Company A's image was its efficiency. This key message was most often communicated in print media and social media, but less frequently across broadcast and online media. As noted on Business Next blog (12/2/09): "It [the product] is the vanguard in Company A's campaign to rebrand product as a brand offering smaller, more efficient products." A highly-rated article in the Sunshine Sentinel (12/18/09) had similar praise for the product's efficiency: "Company A will target young families – buyers who will pay more for a product that has more space, better fuel economy and more premium features than the other products."

Design was the second leading favorable key message, although it did receive some negative commentary. Bolt.com (12/2/09) was one of the social media evangelists, quoting the product's chief designer I Draw Circles, "We wanted to take a big step forward, making a strong design statement for Company A products around the world." The Marietta Times (12/3/09) was less impressed with the design: "And generally the product makes an excellent argument for itself. Except, perhaps, in the matters of exterior styling, where it just lies there like a starfish."

Communications Sources: Company A
by volume, percentage & rating

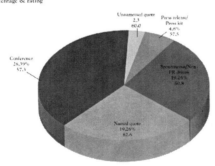

A key driver of the product's positive media rating was the high proportion of PR-driven coverage appearing across media types. Almost half of all product coverage featured input from Company A's proactive outreach, most notably the Convention Center Show (39% of coverage, rated an above-average 57.3). Also driving the product's key messages were the numerous Company A spokespeople quoted – appearing in over one-quarter of all coverage and rating a high 62.6.

Figure 8.2 (cont.). Scorecard with Summarized Bivariate Tables and Stacked Column and Bar Charts.
Used with permission of Echo Research.

Categorical Statistical Analysis

Categorical statistical analysis basically deals with *frequency counts*—the actual number of observations found in each level of a categorical variable. It is important to remember that the frequency count is the basis for all other descriptive statistics, the most common of which is the percentage. A *percentage* is simply the number of observations in a category divided by the total number of observations. Percentage data are often used when the data are to be reported as quartiles (25% segments) or deciles (10% segments). A ratio can be calculated from the frequency counts. A *ratio* is a comparison of two frequencies; for example, say we had 10 males and 5 females, the ratio of males to females would be 2 to 1, stated as 2:1.

Univariate

Univariate descriptive statistics deal with a single variable. For instance, if a content analysis is run with the following categories for story rating, "favorable," "neutral," and "unfavorable," there would be three categories (plus the "other" category, which we will ignore for now). If there are 100 placements, the descriptive statistics might break down as follows: 50 favorable, 30 neutral, and 20 unfavorable. The data can also be described in terms of percentages, with the number of observations per category divided by the total observations: 50% favorable, 30% neutral, and 20% unfavorable. Percentages are often reported with small sample sizes, which may make interpretation difficult. For instance, it seldom happens in large samples that the results come out at 50% or 33.3%, unless they were rounded off. If so, the descriptive analysis should state this. A third descriptive statistic is the ratio. If a survey's results found that males represented 40 out of 400 respondents, while females represented 360 respondents, the proportion of females to males would be 9 to 1, or 9:1.

Visualizing. Categorical descriptive statistics are usually visualized as a univariate table, a bar or column chart (bar charts are horizontal, columns are vertical), or a pie chart, although there are other formats that can be used (e.g., surface, donut, bubble, radar, or spider web).

The following table visually presents the story placement results as a univariate table:

Sex of Respondent		Story Rating	
Female	460	Favorable	50
Male	40	Neutral	30
		Unfavorable	20

Many public relations research firms now provide visualizations of statistics. Several different univariate statistics are visualized in Figures 8.1 and 8.2.

Bivariate and Multivariate

Bivariate and multivariate descriptive statistics describe the relationships between two or more categorical variables. Of the two, bivariate analyses are most common in public relations research reports. A bivariate analysis on the story placement by respondent sex would result in a two column (sex) by three row (story rating) table:

Sex/Story Rating	Female	Male
Favorable	230	20
Neutral	138	12
Unfavorable	92	8
Total	460	40

A multivariate descriptive analysis would produce extra tables. If a third variable were being analyzed, say socioeconomic status of the respondent (low, middle, high), there would be three tables, one for each level of the three variables. In the previous example, we would have a table for low socioeconomic respondents, a table for middle socioeconomic respondents, and a table for high socioeconomic respondents.

Visualizing. Visualizing bivariate and multivariate analyses is typically done through bar or column charts, although the data can be visualized through other types of charts (e.g., pie, spider). Bivariate and multivariate charts are visual representations of a table, as shown in Figures 8.1 and 8.2.

Continuous Statistical Analysis

Continuous data are found on a continuum, hence the label "continuous." Continuous data are considered "stronger" than their categorical counterparts because of the statistical procedures and what they tell researchers. As noted in chapter 3, continuous data are either *interval*, where the distance between data points is considered to be equal, or *ratio*, where the distance between data points is absolute. The demographic variable "age," when calculated from year born, would be interval data (e.g., if I were to respond to a survey question, "In what year were you born?" and filled in 1949, when subtracted from 2009, it would yield my age as 60 years). My bank account, which would be in dollars and cents, would be ratio data.

What makes continuous data so powerful is that along its continuum, the data will fall under some type of curve, which is a function of the distribution of all data points gathered for whatever continuous variable is being examined. All continuous data have their own normal distribution. The hypothetical *normal curve* is shown in Figure 8.3. Of importance is the area under the curve, which can be expressed in "deviations" from the mean or average of all data points. This underlies the concept of continuous data having a *central tendency*—to distribute around that mean. Without going into statistical detail, all data can be demonstrated to fall within *x* number of *standard deviations* (based on the mean and its

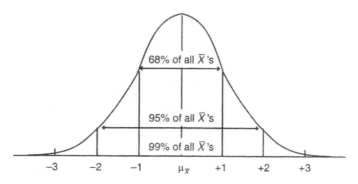

Figure 8.3. The normal curve and standard deviations.

variance, or distribution from the mean). All curves find that 34% of all data will fall 1 standard deviation from the mean, or 68% of the data will fall ±1 standard deviation from the data's mean. This is powerful in terms of description in that it provides much more information than simple frequencies, percentages, or ratios. While there are many continuous statistics available, we will concentrate on six.

Univariate

The five most commonly employed continuous statistics are the mean, median, mode, variance, and standard deviation. The *mean* typically refers to the average of data points for a variable. There are, however, a number of different means used by statisticians,[3] but the mean usually found in public relations research is the average. Means are highly influenced by data points that are extremely far from the average. *Outliers* are data points that influence the mean. Take 10 data points: 1, 2, 3, 4, 5, 6, 7, 8, 9, and 10. The mean for this data set would be 5.5. If one of the data points were an outlier, say instead of 6 it was 22, the mean would be much larger (7.1). When there are outliers, it is essential that the *median*, or the data point that is 50% of the data set scores, be examined. When calculating the median, the data are lined up in order and the middle data point is the mean (for data sets with an even number of data points, the median is the average of the two scores around the 50th percentile). In the case of the 10 scores, the median would be 5.5, same as the mean. In the case of the outlier, the median would be 6.0. The *mode* is the data point(s) that reoccurs most in the data set. In this case, there are no recurring numbers, each number is unique. However, if the data points were 1, 2, 3, 3, 4, 5, 6, 7, 8, 9, the mode would be 3. A data set where the mean, median, and mode are identical would indicate adherence to the hypothetical normal curve, as shown in Figure 8.3. When the mean, median, and mode differ, the shape of the curve flattens. Part of this is due to the variance or distribution of scores.

As noted earlier, all data for a continuous variable are distributed around the mean for that data set. The *variance* provides an indicator of the distribution of data points around the mean. Interestingly, the variance is typically larger for small data sets than larger data sets. Why? Think of an auditorium with 100 seats. The first 10 people come in and find a seat—the distribution will be large, as there are many seats and few people, so their seating may be anywhere. As the number of people increases, the distribution decreases as fewer and fewer seats are left. The variance describes how "normal" the data set is, but it is unique to the data set. The *standard deviation*, which is the square of the variance, normalizes the data and can be used to compare data sets of different variables, even if those variables are measured differently (e.g., 5- or 7-point measure) through the *standardized score* for each variable, which is expressed in terms of the number of standard deviations each score is from the mean. Thus from these continuous statistics, we know the distribution of data around a mean. For instance, the average age for a sample might be 21.2 years, with a standard deviation of 3.2 years. This would tell us that 68% of the sample is 18.0 to 24.4 years old.

Visualizing. Univariate continuous statistics typically are reported as numbers in a table. It is difficult to create a graph of only one variable. When we do, however, we typically find that a line graph is used to visually portray the data (see Figures 8.1 and 8.2). For that we need to turn to bivariate and multivariate variable analyses.

Bivariate and Multivariate

As with categorical variables, more than one variable can be described in relation to another. This is typically done by describing the relationship between means for two or more variables; examining the correlation between the two variables; however, one of those variables must be categorical, which provides points of reference for the analysis. For instance, age and sex can be described by looking at the mean and standard deviation for males and females. When we look at two continuous variables, we typically describe their correlation. A *correlation* is the relationship between the variables data points. A correlation can only reflect the relationship between the two variables, and ranges from a perfect correlation of +1.00 through no correlation at all at 0.00 to a perfect negative correlation of −1.00. According to Hocking, Stacks, and McDermott,[4] correlations below ±.30 are "weak," ±.30 to ±.70 are "moderate," ±.70 to ±.90 are "high," and greater than ±.90 are "very high." In communications research, most correlations are typically less than ±.50, and if higher, they may be restricted by controlling the data range in some way, often making the relationship unclear.

Visualizing. Visualizing bivariate and multivariate relationships is easier than univariate relationships because there is a comparison. The usual visualization is via the line or "fever" graph, with separate lines indicating different variables in relationship to each other (see Figure 8.1). A correlation is visualized as a scatter graph, where one variable is found on the *x*-axis and the other on the *y*-axis. Figure 8.4 shows that the relationship between sales and consumer ratings of an advertisement are positively related. If you were to draw a line through the data points it would go from the lower left corner just above the 6 on the sales axis and continue at an angle upward toward the 6 on the advertisement ratings axis.

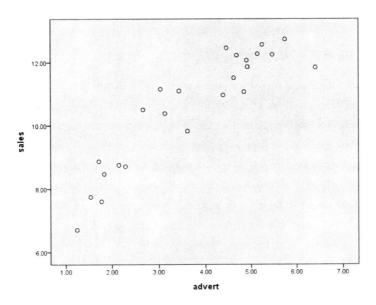

Figure 8.4. Scatter graph.

Using Categorical and Continuous Data to Describe Simple Relationships

Categorical and continuous data are now commonly intermingled in visualizing data from several variables, providing the public relations practitioner with an indication or snapshot of the relationships between variables of interest. Note in the first visual on the second row of Figure 8.1 that some variables are univariate and some are bivariate (and, like comparing means, one axis is categorical and the other continuous).

At this point it is important to emphasize that *descriptive statistics do not analyze the data or the relationships between variables*. To make judgments about variables being larger or smaller than others, or that the relationships are truly "significant," requires that inferences be made. This moves us to a more advanced set of statistics that allows researchers to state the strength of a relationship or lack of relationship within certain degrees of confidence. We turn next to understanding inferential statistical analysis.

Inferential Statistical Analysis

Inferential statistics are seldom reported in public relations research and, if reported, are generally put in footnotes. As a matter of fact, if the study's data represent a true *census* of all respondents or sources, inferential statistics are not needed—any descriptive statistics represent what is found in the study. However, when dealing with larger populations drawn from even larger universes, it is not possible to collect data from all respondents or sources. We then sample, and as we know, certain amounts of error are built into the sampling process. Thus the researcher is left to wonder whether the descriptive statistics are true representations of the larger population and differences among variables are real or whether they are due to chance—or *error*.

One of the reasons survey researchers run inferential statistics on their demographics is to test sampling error. If there were 400 randomly selected respondents to a survey, the researcher is willing to accept up to 5% sampling error—but this does not mean that there was sampling error, just that there might be. Therefore, running inferential tests on the data against known data (and hoping for *no* differences) gives a researcher the ability to say that she is 90%, 95%, or 99% confident that the sample is representative of the larger population. Inferential statistics provide the researcher with a confidence level, or the amount the variables differ from each other.

In survey research, the second form of error is measurement error. Inferential statistics allow us to test for measurement error among the outcome variables when analyzing the descriptive statistics. For instance, if purchase intent of a product is the outcome of interest and the study used measures of product awareness, product knowledge, and liking as indicators of purchase intent, the researcher needs to test whether the variables truly indicate purchase intent, and if so, how much confidence the researcher can have in the results of the tests. The accepted confidence that there are differences is put at 95%. This means that 95 times out of 100 the results obtained are due to the variables indicating purchase intent and not to measurement or other errors.

There are many inferential statistics that can be run on data. Some simply look to see if levels of a categorical variable (e.g., sex) describe differences in the outcome variable. For instance, do males intend to purchase the product more than females, or is the difference in purchase intent due to error? Others try to predict from a number of variables (almost always categorical) that are related to the outcome of interest. For instance, which of three variables, operationalized as dichotomous variables (i.e., high awareness, high knowledge, high liking versus low awareness, knowledge, and liking) best predicts purchase intent? Those statistics that look at differences are fairly simple, and we will look at the chi-square (χ^2) as representative of categorical variables and the t-test and analysis of variance (ANOVA) as representative of continuous tests. Regression is what most use to try to model predictive tests. As noted in the first part of this chapter, it is not our intent to make statisticians out of our readers, but we hope that after the short descriptions that follow you will have a basic understanding of what each test does.

Categorical

The *chi-square* (χ^2) test is one of the most utilized of categorical inferential statistical tests. The chi-square test determines whether the frequency of observations in a given category or level of a variable is different from what would be expected. Chi-square is often used in surveys to test demographic variables against known results, typically against census or industry data. For instance, suppose a random survey of shoppers in a large metropolitan area finds that 56% of the respondents are female and 44% are male. Going to the U.S. Census data (easily available through the U.S. government), we find that for this particular area females constitute 51% of the metropolitan area and males 49%. Chi-square can be used to test the female (56%) and male (44%) data obtained against the census data (51% and 49%, respectively). A chi-square test, if run, would find that the sample differed *significantly* (the probability of differences was confirmed with 95% confidence) from the census data (there is only a 5% chance that the data were due to sampling error).

Continuous

While categorical inferential statistics look for differences between categories, continuous inferential statistics look for differences between means for different categories. The most commonly used inferential test is the *t-test*. The *t*-test looks at differences in continuous outcome variables between variables with two groups (e.g., male/female, high/low, expensive/inexpensive). This is a major limitation, but *t*-tests are easy to interpret. The *t*-test has another limitation—it is sensitive to differences in small samples (less than 150 samples) because of the way it is calculated.[5] Suppose we have two means, male purchase intent on a 5-point scale was found to be 4.5, while female purchase intent was found to be 2.5. The question the *t*-test answers is whether 4.5 is truly different from 2.5 (notice that it is not stated as larger or smaller, but as different). A *t*-test run on the means would find that, yes, the two groups are significantly different and that the researcher can be 95% confident in making that claim.

For larger samples, or for studies where there are more than two levels of a variable or more than one variable, a different test is run. The *analysis of variance* (ANOVA) or *F-test* is a more general test that is not sensitized to large samples. Instead of using a special variance measure, it simply looks for the variance that can be explained by being in a category (high, moderate, low awareness) as compared against the variance of being in any group (called "between-group" or systematic variance for the category and "within-group" or error variance for all respondents across groups) for the outcome variable (purchase intent). The ANOVA then tests to see if there is less variance for groups as compared against all respondents. With a larger sample, the results for dichotomous variables are similar to the t-test. However, with three or more groups, a significant overall finding (that being in a group did make a difference in the outcome variable) does not indicate how the groups differed. In that case, more tests must be run, which are a specialized form of the ANOVA—the ONE-WAY ANOVA.[6]

Finally, there are times when researchers want to predict which variables best predict an outcome. The most commonly used statistical test for this purpose is a simple or multiple regression. The regression first looks for differences between variables and then looks for how the variables correlate. By drawing a line through the correlation matrix, outcomes can be predicted for individual variables or you can test to see which variables of several will best predict outcomes.[7] The variables that are examined are the "dependent variable" and the "independent variables," which impact or affect the dependent variable. An example of a dependent variable is "willingness to purchase" a product or service. What regression does is examine a series of other variables that impact or "drive" a "willingness to purchase" and determine the overall contribution each of these independent variables on that decision. Examples of independent variables include overall awareness of a product, levels of knowledge about the product, or affinity toward or prior relationship between the company and the purchaser.

Best Practices

Best practices public relations employs descriptive and inferential statistics in analyzing the effect of public relations variables on the outcomes of interest. Running appropriate statistical tests and being able to discuss the descriptive findings is the first step in best practices statistical analysis. The second step is to run the appropriate inferential statistics to test for confidence in those differences and which variables best predict specific outcomes.

Summary

Continuous inferential statistics are powerful tests of differences between and potential predictors of variables relating to some outcome. With the increased emphasis on proving value, public relations research is moving quickly to employing more inferential tests. In many instances, public relations researchers do employ inferential tests, but to simplify presentations and final reports, they are often not included. The inferential test provides the public relations professional with the information necessary to state with confidence whether or not variables in a program or campaign are effective in demonstrating return on expectations, and ultimately return on investment.

CHAPTER 9

Sampling

One of the most significant challenges in any form of research is ensuring that respondents participating in a study are the right individuals. This process begins with the stating of study objectives, where we define the research and information needs, and, in turn, determine which stakeholder group is the most appropriate audience. As noted in chapter 7, these individuals can be defined in a multitude of ways that range from simple demographic descriptions, such women who are 18 to 34 years old, to complex definitions that incorporate geographic, demographic, and attitudinal characteristics.

Regardless of whether the description is simple or complex, the challenge remains the same for the researcher. That challenge is ensuring that those selected for inclusion in a study are representative of the larger universe of individuals who constitute the group that is the focus of the study. A representative group of study participants is crucial since the findings from the study will be used to make decisions about the direction of a communications program, evaluate the success or failure of that program, or determine adjustments or modifications that need to take place in order to ensure communications and business objectives are being met. Without a sample that represents the broad opinions of the stakeholder group under study, it is highly likely that the essential decisions that are based on the research will be in error.

Why Do We Need to Sample?

In an ideal situation, we would ask each and every member of the population their opinions. We would ask them what they like and dislike, what they are aware of, and what their expectations are. That approach would, in theory, be error free, since everyone's opinion would be included and all subgroups, by definition, would be represented in their correct proportions in the overall population—this called a *census*. The practical reality is, however, that speaking to *every possible respondent* is a practical impossibility. Using that approach, a study employing a census of the adult population of the United States would require more than 230 million individual interviews.[1] A study of that magnitude would take years of planning, months to complete, and millions of dollars. Decisions on communications programs often need information that can be collected and analyzed in as little as a few days and rarely longer than a few weeks time. These limitations render a census approach to survey research impractical except in very limited instances where an entire population is available for study and has a strong willingness to cooperate with the survey. An example of this type of research is an employee survey.

The solution is to talk to a group of individuals who are selected in a manner that ensures that their opinions are representative of the broader population. This approach is called *sampling*, which is based on the assumption that individuals who have shared or common characteristics, such as demographic variables like age, gender, income, or marital status, also are likely to share opinions or preferences because they are likely to have similar backgrounds, interests, and lifestyles. The same is assumed to be true for psychographics (their attitudinal preferences) and netgraphics (their use of the Internet or Internet-based Communications; see chapter 7). This method reduces the cost as well as the time required to complete a reliable survey, but unlike a census or the inclusion of all eligible respondents, it is subject to a certain margin of error.

Before we look at the two major types of sampling it is important to determine what the study's sampling frame will be. In chapter 7 the *sampling frame* was introduced as a way to ensure that the respondents selected for study would reflect the purposes of that study. In general, the sampling frame defines who is to be sampled from the universe of all possible respondents, reduced to the population (or public or audience) being examined, and further reduced to the sample itself. The *sampling frame* does exactly what it implies: it frames the sample's respondents to particular demographic, psychographic, or netgraphic variables. Further, from secondary research the researcher should know the percentage or proportion of the population, public, or audience and, upon collecting data, be able to compare the sample's breakdown against the population to check sampling reliability and validity.[2]

The next section covers the two basic types of sampling used in research, explaining each type and providing methods within each. The section following that is more hands-on and walks through how an actual sample might be drawn. We turn next to the types of sampling.

Types of Sampling

Sampling can generally be divided into two basic types: probability and nonprobability. *Probability sampling* is used to make reliable and project-able predictions about the attitudes and opinions of an entire population being studied. Probability sampling has a unique benefit in that sampling error or the degree to which the attitudes, opinions, or preferences of a sample may differ from a population as a whole can be calculated. This error is commonly reported as a *plus-or-minus sampling error*. This allows the researcher to "know" how much sampling error and measurement error can be *expected* and how much the researcher is willing to *allow*.

Sampling and Measurement Error

Sampling error occurs for a variety of reasons, but most often it involves sampling frame, list, or measurement error. First, if the sample frame is not specified exactly enough, there will be *sampling frame error* due to the inability to correctly frame or correctly identify the population under study. Second, there may be list errors. *List errors* occur when the contact lists—telephone books, voting records, purchaser data, and so forth—are not correct or have lapsed. Thus while the sample frame may be fine, the list of respondents contains error. Third, *measurement errors* come from respondents misunderstanding a question or statement.

Chapter 8 introduced the concept of the *normal curve*. It is this statistical concept that allows researchers to estimate how much error in sampling and measurement can be expected. The amount of error is decreased as the sample size increases because, as sample size increases, the data gathered become more equally distributed and approach what would be normally found in the population. This is not to imply that a perfect sample would have no error—*there is always some error*—but we seek to minimize it. Without going into a lot of statistical formulas, if a sample needs to be at least 95% correct and the researcher is willing to accept up to 5% measurement error, then about 400 (438 actually) randomly sampled respondents from the population would be required. Reducing measurement error to 1% would require 9,604 respondents. And to get 1% sampling error (99% sample confidence) and 5% measurement error, you would need 663 randomly selected respondents.[3] If it cost $100 per completed response, you can see where trade-offs in terms of expected error come into play.

Nonprobability sampling, by definition, cannot be projected to reflect the attitudes or opinions of a specific population group. In essence, the degree to which the sample differs from the population remains unknown. Nonetheless, this method is a valuable form of sampling that can provide insights and understanding of what a target population thinks and how they behave. What needs to be remembered and stressed in the final report of the study is that results cannot be generalized away from the actual sample itself. In other words, the nonprobability sample yields a descriptive rather than a projective study.

Probability Sampling

Probability sampling takes several different forms: *random sampling*, *systemic sampling*, and *stratified sampling*. While each of these forms of sampling is distinct, they have a common element that links them. The common linkage is that in each form of probability sampling, every prospective respondent to a survey has an equal chance or a "nonzero probability" of being selected for a survey.

Random sampling is the most elemental and basic form of probability sampling. In this method, each member of the surveyed population has an equal and known chance of being selected.

In *systematic sampling*, also called "*n*th name selection." the sample size is calculated and every "*n*th" record is selected from a list of population members, thus distributing the selected respondents throughout the list. This method is less robust and reliable than a purely random sample and has the potential to create a biased sample if the list used to select respondents is ordered in a hidden or unknown way. This approach is useful when there is a limited population to be interviewed, but where the population is too large to be effectively and efficiently studied using a census approach.

Stratified sampling is a common sampling method when there is a known subset of a population under study that is important to include in the final analysis, but where the population of that subgroup is too small to appear in sufficient numbers in a purely random sample and still allow for a meaningful analysis. An example of a subset that would be used in a stratified sample would be large businesses. In a study of 500 randomly selected businesses, normally only 10 to 20 of these businesses might be present in the final sample. In this instance, the researcher would specify a subsample of 100 of these large businesses in order to have an analyzable segment. Random sampling is used to select a sufficient number of subjects from each subgroup. The final sample is adjusted statistically to make sure large businesses are present in their correct proportion or a separate and statistically reliable analysis of this subgroup could also be conducted.

A special form of stratified sampling is the *systematic stratified sample*. In this case respondents are randomly selected by either the nth record method or simple random sampling, but are stratified within a particular variable, say, the respondents sex, where a certain number of males and a certain number of females would be randomly selected.

Nonprobability Sampling

As in probability sampling, there are several approaches to nonprobability studies. There are four basic variations of nonprobability sampling: *convenience sampling, judgment sampling, quota sampling,* and *snowball sampling.* By definition, nonprobability sampling does not support projections or generalization of the survey findings to a broader population or census. Nonetheless, it remains a useful tool when there are specialty populations that are of limited size, respondents that are hard to reach, or circumstances where traditional probability approaches would be prohibitive in terms of the cost and the time required to complete the study.

Convenience sampling is typically used in exploratory research. In this instance, respondents are selected for inclusion in the sample because they are convenient and easy to reach. Researchers often use this approach when they are looking for a "rough" approximation and are also looking to minimize cost and the time required to conduct a probability study. This approach is also commonly used in qualitative research, particularly in the selection of respondents for participation in focus groups. In this instance, respondents are recruited from databases and have already indicated a willingness to participate in a research study. Another instance where convenience sampling is used is with mall intercept studies. These studies recruit respondents from shopping malls, where interviewers solicit the respondents' cooperation.

Judgment sampling is a variation of convenience sampling that often combines nonprobability and probability sampling. In a judgment sample, a single city or a neighborhood could be chosen to represent a wider population. In this case, the respondents within the area are chosen randomly using probability techniques. This type of sampling is often used for "exit polling" during political elections, relying on "sample precincts" to predict election outcomes. These sample precincts are selected based on prior voter behavior and are likely to be indicative of actual voter preferences. Another use of judgment sampling is in "test markets," where specific cities or neighborhoods are selected to determine if a product has broad appeal prior to a national introduction. In both instances, substantial background research is required in order to make an informed decision of which markets are to be included in the study.

A variation of the judgment sample approach is *cluster sampling*. In cluster sampling an entire population is divided into groups, or clusters, and a random sample of these clusters is selected for inclusion in the study. For example, this method is used when a broad, geographically diverse population is under study. Under these circumstances, it is often expensive and time consuming to conduct a random study. Therefore a geographic "cluster" of respondents is used to represent the larger population. This approach can be used in probability and nonprobability sampling. Caution should be exercised with this method because overall error rates are significantly higher than with traditional sampling methods.

Quota sampling is similar to stratified sampling in that the objective of the sampling approach is to ensure specific groups are represented in sufficient numbers in order to be analyzed. These groups are predetermined by the researcher who determines the desired sample. The final quota sample is then selected using convenience or judgment sampling methods. Like other forms of nonprobability sampling, the findings from quota samples cannot be projected to a larger population.

When a respondent group is particularly difficult to reach, one solution is to use a procedure called *snowball sampling*. One of the challenges when a respondent group is rare or low incidence in the overall population is that it can be cost prohibitive to locate respondents. Snowball sampling asks for referrals from initial subjects to generate additional subjects. An example of snowball sampling may be identifying individuals with a rare or unusual disease. Two factors influence the difficulty in finding these respondents. In one instance, there are few of these individuals in the overall population. Adding to this difficulty are privacy laws that limit access through third parties. It is not unusual, however, for those who have a specific condition to know others who have the same condition. They often meet in support groups and forge relationships that can lead to referrals. While this approach can quickly build samples, it is also fraught with the danger that the sample will be biased because it does not represent a true cross section of the overall population under study.

Sampling Applications

Chapter 7 reviewed the various types of survey methods. For each of these methods there are specific factors that need to be considered when developing a sample to ensure the results of the survey are reliable.

Telephone Surveys

The most common sampling system used in telephone surveys is a probability method called *random digit dialing* (RDD). The RDD method randomly selects telephone numbers from known working residential or business telephone exchanges. The RDD approach is used since it includes listed and unlisted telephone numbers in their correct proportions. Currently about 30% of households have an unlisted telephone number; this method ensures their inclusion in a study. Further randomization is added to the study by requesting to speak to a resident at random. One method for selecting that individual is asking for the adult in the household who had the most recent birthday.

The RDD approach is becoming increasingly difficult to use because of the rapid growth of cell phones as a primary means of telephonic communication. Cell phones are now in a high percentage of households, and this percentage is increasing rapidly, particularly among younger adults. These numbers are not included in samples and therefore a significant bias is created because younger adults are most likely to be excluded from the sample.

In some instances, nonprobability samples are used in telephone studies. These are referred to as "list samples." These samples are typically drawn from directories or similar sources. This type of sampling approach is most commonly used when respondents have special characteristics (e.g., ownership or use of a particular type of product) or are a low-incidence group in the population and therefore are difficult to reach through conventional random dialing. An example of a low-incidence group would be owners of small retail businesses. This nonprobability approach is significantly more cost effective than random respondent selection.

Door-to-Door Surveys

This approach is the "original" probability sampling method and continues to be the "gold standard" of sampling. In door-to-door surveys, households are randomly selected from known clusters. This selection is based on known addresses. The database of known residences is available from the U.S. Postal Service (USPS). The USPS is responsible for delivering to all known households and therefore is required to maintain these lists and keep them updated.

While this approach is highly reliable, it is time consuming and extremely expensive. Consequently it is rarely used except in rare circumstances where the nature of the questions requires an in-person interview as well as projectability to a larger population.

Online Studies

Online studies are, by definition, nonprobability studies since respondents are usually part of a panel of individuals who have agreed in advance to respond to a series of surveys in exchange for compensation or gifts. In many instances the final sample is "weighted" to ensure that respondents in various demographic groups are present in the correct proportions for the overall population. Weighting is a process that uses "correction factors" or weights to place each segment of the population in their correct proportions in the final sample. This process is used to approximate probability sampling methods; however, significant debate continues on the ability of this approach to provide reliable projections. The method is increasingly popular, however, since the research can be completed quite quickly and at considerably lower costs than traditional telephone or door-to-door studies. These interviewing systems are becoming increasingly sophisticated and respondents can be questioned without leaving their computers.

Intercept Studies

Intercept studies are nonprobability studies that are used when it is necessary to conduct in-person interviews and the time or cost required for a door-to-door study is prohibitive. Most shopping malls have exclusive research services that identify potential survey respondents that they invite to participate in a study. They are not selected randomly, but by their willingness to cooperate with the administration of an interview, and they are not necessarily representative of a larger population because they are engaged in an activity (shopping) that may distinguish them from the overall population. Consequently their opinions could differ considerably from others. This approach is commonly used when communications materials are being tested for efficacy since it is easy to show an individual test materials and is relatively inexpensive.

Content Analysis

In addition to survey applications, probability sampling can also be used in content analysis (see chapter 6). Sampling is used to randomly select articles for inclusion in an analysis when the overall volume of articles is too large to analyze efficiently. In some instances, thousands of articles may be generated, making it difficult to provide prompt and timely reporting of the findings. In this instance, articles are randomly selected using a random-number generator. This method determines which articles in a group of articles are chosen for deeper study and analysis.

Stratified sampling can also be used in content analysis. In this case, specific media that are particularly important are selected separately to ensure that adequate proportions are available for analysis.

Drawing a Sample

To this point the discussion has been theoretical; we have looked at what sampling *is* (census, probability, and nonprobability). To better understand the various sampling options, this section discusses the process of sampling for specific types of studies that typically may be conducted as part of a communications program.

Census

A census includes each and every individual who is eligible for a study according to the specified sampling frame. The challenge of a census is to systematically ensure that each and every individual who is eligible actively participates in the study. The only practical applications of a

Table 9.1. Applications for Each Form of Sampling

Type of Data Collection	Probability Sample	Nonprobability Sample
Telephone	✓	✓
Door-to-Door	✓	
Online		✓
Intercept		✓
Content Analysis	✓	✓

census are for very small populations, such as employees of a small or midsize company or similar types of populations. The other use of a census approach is for content analysis, where it may be practical to include every available story in an analysis.

National Telephone Study

There are two general approaches for conducting a telephone study. One approach is called a *listed sample* or *directory* approach. An example of this method would start with a list or directory of all areas where the study is to take place. Names and their associated telephone numbers are randomly selected for the study. This approach has significant limits. This approach is time and labor intensive, and it also has several significant flaws that limit the ability of the study to be representative of the population being studied. One flaw is that significant proportions of eligible respondents may not be included in the study. Those with unlisted telephone numbers, as well as those with new or recent listings, will not be included. In some localities, this could represent 3 in 10 potential respondents.

One of the solutions to this problem is something called the *modified Waksberg method* of RDD.[4] In this approach, clusters of known and working residential telephone exchanges are identified. A sample of these working exchanges is selected and telephone numbers that include the digits that comprise the exchange are generated. The last two digits of the number are randomly generated. This procedure ensures that all working telephone numbers (listed, unlisted, and new listings) have an equal opportunity of appearing in the final study. Statistical adjustments are often applied to the final sample to ensure that all demographic groups appear in their correct proportions.

Intercept Study

Since intercept studies are nonprobability studies, sampling issues focus on the sampling frame rather than the sampling method. In this type of data collection, the key to ensuring the sample meets the specifications for the study lies in determining those characteristics that are desired for the respondents and creating a questionnaire that determines if prospective respondents are eligible to participate. This process, called *screening*, is similar to the screening process for focus groups described in chapter 5.

In an intercept study, prospective respondents are often identified visually by an interviewer who approaches these individuals according to specified instructions (e.g., men 18 to 34 years old, or young women who are shopping for new clothes). The individuals are then asked a series of study qualification questions to determine if they are eligible to participate in the study. If the individual is eligible, that person is asked to participate in the full study. In some mall intercept studies, quotas are set for specific types of respondents. For example, as study design may require subsamples of different age groups. Once these quotas are filled, respondents in those groups are no longer eligible to participate in the study even though they meet all other qualifications for inclusion.

Online Study

Online studies present unique challenges in drawing or developing samples. Respondents to online studies are usually members of panels of individuals who have been "prequalified" for participation in studies based on known characteristics. These characteristics include demographic variables such as gender, age, occupation, or education, as well as other variables such as product ownership or use and even the use of medication or the presence of specific medical conditions. Typically they have agreed in advance to participate in studies in exchange for compensation and are regular Internet users. They are often recruited from websites and e-mail solicitations, as well as referrals from other panelists. All of these factors are variables that make it challenging to project the findings from this type of research to broader populations.

The most common sampling approach used for online studies is a random selection of panelists who receive invitations to participate in a particular study. They are selected based on their answers to earlier studies, but are usually "requalified" for new studies. The invitations are often sent over several days to avoid potential biases associated with those who respond early. As in telephone studies, statistical adjustments are often applied to the final sample to ensure all demographic groups appear in their correct proportions.

Content Analysis

Most content analysis uses a census approach. However, in some instances it is impractical to include every article in an analysis. There are two procedures that are used to determine which articles are analyzed as part of a study.

One approach is a random selection of articles. In this approach, the total number of articles to be included in the analysis is determined. This determination is made based on the overall budget to conduct the analysis, the time required, or a combination of these factors. Two different random selections can be applied. One is the nth selection process, where every nth article is selected. The other approach is a random selection of articles.

The n is determined by the total number of articles in the census divided by the number of articles to be included in the analysis. This process yields an equal distribution throughout the list of articles. Ideally the articles would be listed in an organized structure, most often chronologically, which helps minimize bias in the selection process.

The random selection is determined by a *random-number generator*. A random-number generator is a device that generates a sequence of numbers that lack any pattern. Articles are organized in a sequence similar to that used in the nth selection process and are numbered sequentially. Articles are selected according to the random number generated by matching that number to the article with the same number. Random-number generators are available on numerous websites.

Another approach to content analysis sampling is to limit the number of articles to specific criteria. These criteria include the types of publications or media outlets included and specific content of the articles; for example, earnings reports on companies may be excluded from a study, or at least two mentions of a company may be required for the article to be included. Articles can also be limited to specific publications or categories of publications, such as daily newspapers or weekly news magazines.

Best Practices

Best practices sampling takes into account the type of sampling required for the research. It begins with an understanding of the universe of possible respondents, defines that universe down to a particular population, and sets a sampling frame. The particular kind of sample generated will depend on what the goals and objectives of the research are. Best practices sampling *reports* include the number of respondents sampled, how they were sampled, and the measurement error associated with the sampling.

Summary

Sampling is an important element of public relations research. Whether a sample is drawn randomly or not, sampling allows the researcher to conduct a study with a smaller number of respondents or participants within certain expectations of error in sampling and measurement. Even in a nonprobability sample, a comparison against expected demographic variables provides some estimate of sampling error, and with a large enough sample (at least 400), some idea of measurement error within the sample can be estimated. Finally, sampling goes beyond the survey or poll and can be used in experiments and even in content analysis. Understanding sampling and the advantages and limitations of each type of sampling provides the researcher with a way to ascertain in secondary research whether the study being reviewed is a reliable and valid document that can be used to help define developmental and refinement phases of a public relations campaign or program.

PART IV

Wrapping Up

Part IV wraps up and reviews the key factors that need to be considered when conducting public relations research, measurement and evaluation. Part IV places in context the key information from parts I, II, and III and presents a series of nine best research and measurement practices based upon these parts that form the foundation for creating communications programs that are effective in achieving their goals. The part includes a review on setting objectives, the use of specific research methods and the applications of a research, measurement and evaluation program.

CHAPTER 10

Best Practices in Public Relations Research, Measurement, and Evaluation[1]

Companies specializing in public relations measurement and evaluation have traditionally focused on evaluating only the outcomes of public relations. These outcomes are most commonly the media or press coverage that is a direct result of media relations activities (outputs). The primary limitation of these companies is their limited focus on an intermediary in the public relations process—the media—rather than on the target audience for these communications activities.

Relying strictly on evaluations of intermediaries in the communications process fails to create effective measurement and evaluation systems that provide a diagnostic appraisal of communications activities, which, in turn, can lead to enhanced communications performance. The failure to include diagnostic measures ignores one of the fundamental "best practices" in communications research and is the key reason why public relations measurement and evaluation has failed to progress significantly over the past 25 years.

Best Practices in Public Relations Research

In public relations research, there are nine best practices that can serve as the foundation for establishing a standardized set of measures for public relations activities. These practices are divided between two broad areas: (1) the use of specific research methods and procedures, and (2) the application of measures that examine both the quality and the substance of public relations activities.

Research Methods and Procedures

There are three research methods and procedures that are an essential part of best practices in public relations research. These methods and procedures include every key step in the research process, from the inception of the project through the delivery of the research report itself. These three steps are

1. Setting clear and well-defined research objectives;
2. Applying rigorous research design that meets the highest standards of research methods and ensures reliable research results; and
3. Providing detailed supporting documentation with full transparency.

Clear and Well-Defined Research Objectives

Setting clear and well-defined research objectives is the critical first step in the public relations research process. Unfortunately it is the aspect of best research practices that is typically either overlooked or not given the level of attention that it requires in order to create an effective and reliable measurement and evaluation system. The establishment of clear and well-defined definitions is particularly critical because research objectives function as the foundation upon which the rest of the research program rests.[2] The key to setting these objectives so they can effectively contribute to a measurement and evaluation program that meets best standards involves answering the following five questions:

- *Is the information need clearly articulated?*
  In order for any form of measurement and evaluation to be effective, it is essential that the information be specific and unambiguous. A generalized information need such as "How well did the program perform?" is unlikely to serve as an effective basis for any research-based decisions. The more appropriate questions are "What is the level of awareness of the product, issue or situation?" "How knowledgeable is the target audience about the material being communicated?" "Is the information relevant to the target audience?" "How has the attitude of the audience been impacted by exposure to communications?" "Is the target audience willing to take any form of action as a result of exposure to

the communications program?" These questions result in setting specific information objectives that can be reliably measured and provide data that can be used to improve communications performance.

- *Are the target audiences for the communications program well defined?*

  It is essential to understand who the *target audience* is as precisely as possible.[3] This is important for several reasons. The primary reason is practical. In order to conduct research that reliably measures and evaluates a communications program, it is essential that those to whom the program is directed also serve as the source of the information about the audience. A poorly defined audience is typically one that is so broad in its scope that it includes those unlikely to express an interest or need. An example of an audience that may be too broad in its scope is "women age 18 to 49 years old." In contrast, a more narrowly defined audience is "mothers of children that are 12 years of age or younger." While the former group includes the latter group, it is less precise, and depending on the product or service, less likely to yield the same information.

- *Are business objectives being met through the information gathered from the research?*

  The central reason for conducting any type of measurement and evaluation research is to address a business issue or concern. Consequently, as the objectives for the research are being established, it is critical that a detailed assessment of the business take place as a first step in the process. For example, if the issue is assessing the introduction of a new product category, then measuring awareness is highly relevant and essential. However, if the business issue concerns a prominent national brand, then purchase intent may be a more relevant and important measure to include in the research program. The more closely research is tied to delivering business objectives, the more valuable and strategic it will be.

- *Is there a plan for how the findings from the research will be used?*

  Just as it is important to have a clear understanding of the research objectives, it is equally essential to understand the types of actions that can be taken as a direct result of the information that is gathered in the research process. The intent is to create research that functions as an aid in the decision-making process rather than having it serve as an end in and of itself. For this reason, it is best to consider likely internal users or "customers" for the research findings at the outset (e.g., marketing, investor relations, new product development, human resources, market or business units). Human nature being what it is, it is also advisable to secure their involvement and buy-in first, so that the findings are welcomed and applied constructively, not just as an afterthought. Objective "listening" research and the insights derived from it are tremendously powerful in terms of internal education for management and an appreciation for the strategic focus of communications.

- *Is the organization prepared to take action based on research findings?*

  Just as important as having a plan for applying the research is having an understanding of the actions the organization is willing to take based on the findings. If the senior decision makers are unwilling to undertake specific actions, then creating a research program that measures and evaluates that action will have little value to the organization and may actually be counterproductive to the organization's long-term goals and objectives.

Rigorous Research Design

Once objectives have been established, it is important to design research that both supports the objectives and is rigorous enough to provide usable and actionable information. This rigor not only ensures reliable research results, but also provides a foundation for measuring and evaluating communications performance over time. Again, a series of nine questions needs to addressed in order to ensure that rigorous research designs are applied.

- *Is the sample well defined?*

  The research sample, just like the target audience, needs to be precisely defined in order to make sure it is the actual target audience for communications that is included in the research. The recommended approach is to screen potential research respondents for these defining characteristics before beginning the study. These defining characteristics can be demographic (e.g., age, gender, education, occupation, region, etc.), job title or function, attitudes, product use, or any combination of these. However, while it is important to define the sample precisely, caution must also be exercised to make sure that key members of the target group are included in the sample. In some instances, samples require minimal quotas of specific types of respondents in order to ensure that analyzable segments of each quota group are included in the study.

- *Are respondents randomly selected?*

  One of the most significant and immeasurable biases that can occur in a study is the exclusion of potential respondents who are difficult to reach and therefore are less likely to participate in the study. Special attention needs to be paid to ensure that these individuals have an equal opportunity to participate. This is typically accomplished through multiple contacts over an extended period with a random sample or replica of the group being studied. It is also essential to be sensitive to the audience being studied and appropriately adapt the ways that responses to questions are secured. Examples of these very specific groups of individuals that require increased sensitivity are young children or other groups where there are special laws and regulations guiding data collection, night shift workers, ethnic minorities, and disabled or disadvantaged groups. (See chapter 9 for a detailed discussion of sampling.)

- *Are appropriate sample sizes used?*

  Samples need to provide reliability in two ways. The primary need is to make certain the overall sample is statistically reliable. The size of the sample can vary considerably, from a few hundred respondents to more than 1,000 individuals. The decision to use one sample size over another is contingent on the size of the overall population represented by the sample, as well as the number of subgroups that will be included in the analysis. For example, a national study of Americans typically requires a sample of 1,000 respondents. This ensures geographic and demographic diversity, as well as adequately sized subgroups between which reliable comparisons can be made. In contrast, a survey of senior executives may require only 200 to 400 completed interviews in order to meet its objectives.

- *Are the appropriate statistical tests used?*

  Survey research is subject to sampling error. This error is typically expressed as a range of accuracy. A number of different standards can be applied to determine this level of accuracy, as well as serve as the basis to compare findings between surveys. The most common standard used is the 95% measure. This standard ensures that the findings, in 19 out of 20 cases, will be reliable within a specific error range for both sampling and measurement. This error range varies depending on the size of the sample under consideration, with a larger sample providing a correspondingly smaller range of error. With that standard in place, a number of different statistical tests can be applied. The key is to select the proper test for the situation being tested. (See chapter 8 for a detailed discussion of statistical testing.)

- *Is the data collection instrument unbiased?*

  A questionnaire can impact the results of a survey in much the same way as the sample selection procedures. The wording and sequence of questions can significantly influence results. Therefore it is essential to make sure that the wording and

structure of the questionnaire is unbiased and does not influence how a respondent answers a question. Paying attention
to this concern increases the reliability of the findings and
provides a better basis for decision making.

- *Are the data tabulated correctly?*

  Special care needs to be taken to make sure that the responses
  from each questionnaire are properly entered into an analytic system so that data from the entire study can be reliably
  tabulated. Data should be entered into a database, with each
  questionnaire functioning as an independent record. This will
  allow for subsequent verification if errors are detected and will
  also allow for the greatest analytic flexibility. Accuracy will also
  be significantly enhanced with this approach. Spreadsheets do
  not provide the same analytic flexibility as specialized statistical packages (i.e., SAS or IBM® SPSS® Statistics) and it is
  significantly harder to detect errors when using these types of
  data entry systems.

- *Are the data presented accurately?*

  Assuming the data are tabulated properly, it is equally important that they be presented in a manner that accurately represents the findings. While data are often selectively presented,
  the omission of data should not be allowed if they present
  misleading or inaccurate results. Consequently the full data
  set needs to be available, even if the data are only selectively
  presented.

- *Is qualitative research used appropriately?*

  Well-executed qualitative research (focus groups, individual
  in-depth interviews, and participant observation) can provide
  unique insights that are not available from other sources.
  While these insights are invaluable, this form of research is not
  a substitute for survey data. Qualitative research is particularly
  useful in three applications: development of communications
  messages, testing and refinement of survey research tools, and

providing insights as well as deeper explanations of survey findings. (See chapter 5 for a detailed discussion of qualitative research
methods.)

- *Can the study findings be replicated through independent testing?*

  If research is properly executed, reproducing the study should
  yield similar results. The only exception is when significant communications activity has occurred that will impact attitudes and
  opinions. Unless the study is reliably constructed so that it can be
  replicated, it will be difficult to produce studies that can be reliably
  compared and which will demonstrate the actual impact of communications activities. (See chapter 7 for a detailed discussion of
  experimental design.)

Detailed Supporting Documentation

While it is essential to employ a rigorous research design when measuring and
evaluating public relations activities, it is just as critical to document how the
research was conducted. This documentation provides a clear understanding
of the issues being measured and a detailed description of the audience being
studied. Just as important, it provides the information required to replicate
the study so that consistent measurement and evaluation can be applied.
Three questions need to be answered to ensure that the documentation meets
the standards of best practices:

- *Is the research method described fully?*

  The description of the method includes not only *how* the study
  was conducted (telephone, in person, online, etc.), but also the
  time frame when the interviews took place, *who* conducted the
  interviews, and a description of the *sample.*

- *Is the questionnaire—as well as any other data collection
  instruments—available for review?*

  This ensures that the reader understands the context of the questions by being able to refer back to the questionnaire when reviewing the data set. It also allows for easier replication of the study.

- *Is the full data set available if requested?*

  Availability of the data provides full transparency of the findings as well as the foundation for doing comparative analyses with subsequent waves of the research. It also allows for additional tabulation of the data and other analyses that may be useful in a subsequent analysis.

Quality and Substance of Research Findings

The second broad area contributing to best practices in public relations research involves six practices that ensure the research findings contribute to improving communications programs:

1. Designing the research to demonstrate the effectiveness of public relations activities
2. Linking public relations outputs to outcomes
3. Using the findings to aid in the development of better communications programs
4. Demonstrating an impact on business outcomes;
5. Being cost effective
6. Having applicability to a broad range of public relations activities

Demonstrating Effectiveness

The central reason to conduct measurement and evaluation research is to determine if a communications program works. Consequently every set of research objectives and each research design needs to ask the following questions:

- *Is the research designed to show the potential impact of a message, program, or campaign?*

  This is the primary "acid test" when designing a measurement and evaluation effort. Unless the research has this capability built into the design, it should be reconsidered. These designs can vary considerably from situation to situation. However, a common element of many measurement and evaluation programs is setting a baseline or benchmark at the initial stages of the research and using that benchmark as the basis for evaluating performance, preferably throughout the campaign at specified intervals.

- *Is the research designed to function as a benchmark to gauge future performance?*

  A benchmark study has to examine basic communications measures. The importance of each of the measures may vary over time. However, basic measures of awareness, knowledge, interest or relevance, and intent to take action need to be considered for inclusion in most studies.

Linking Outputs to Outcomes

A significant proportion of public relations measurement and evaluation focuses attention on the evaluation of media placements. While media placements are often critical in the evaluation and measurement process, they represent only one limited aspect of the public relations process. More importantly, concentrating analysis on only that one area fails to take into account the fundamental issue that public relations activities take place in order to impact a target audience. While the media are a key target for this activity, they actually function as an intermediary or conduit. The fundamental question that needs to be asked is

- *Does the research examine the entire public relations process?*

  This process needs to include an examination of the program's communications objectives and media placement, as well as the impact of these placements on the target audience.

Developing Better Communications Programs

The goal of a measurement and evaluation program is not to determine the success or failure of a public relations program. The goal is to improve the overall performance of these efforts.

There are two best practices that need to be applied:

- *Is a diagnostic element built into the research that provides insight and direction to improve program performance?*

  Research needs to do more than measure communications performance. It also needs to provide insight into the communications objectives and the target audiences. Consequently the research needs to offer direction for public relations programs and their content and identify corrective strategies so the programs achieve their goals. Measurement in this instance is not an end in itself. Rather it is a diagnostic, feedback-oriented tool.

- *Is research conducted early in the program to take advantage of the information?*

  Ideally measurement and evaluation should take place at the beginning of a communications program so that the findings can be incorporated into the program's planning and strategy. The benefit of this research is lost if the only research conducted takes place at the end of the effort.

Demonstrating Impact on Business Outcomes

While a more effective communications program is a central reason to conduct research, the real goal is to have a demonstrable impact on business objectives. The key questions that need to be asked about the research design need to concentrate on evaluating communications performance—outcomes—and mediating variables, such as reputation and relationships (and trust and transparency), on business outcomes.[4] An important aspect of research is establishing appropriate benchmarks and building in key performance indicators:

- *Did the product sell (outcome); were attitudes changed (outtake); did reputations improve as a direct result of the public relations program (outcome)?*[5]

  Each of these is a specific business outcome that has an impact on the operations of an organization. It is essential to determine if it is the program that affected these changes or if it was some other action.

- *How did the public relations effort contribute to overall success?*

    If the public relations program contributed to these changes and shifts, then it is equally important to determine which elements of the program had the greatest impacts (correspondence between outputs and outcomes).

As the chart in Figure 10.1 illustrates, there is a strong interrelationship between the organization setting the communications objectives, messages sent by the organization, how those messages are received, and how the out-takes from those messages impact the objectives set by the organization.

Cost-Effectiveness

There are a number of formulas that provide guidelines for the proportion of a public relations budget that should be devoted to measurement and evaluation. The issue, however, is not about how much should be spent, but if the inclusion of research in the program increased effectiveness—that it has a value that is greater than the cost of the actual research.

- *Did the research enhance the effectiveness of the public relations effort?*

    This is the first question that needs to be answered. If the program did not improve as a result of the research, or if the information

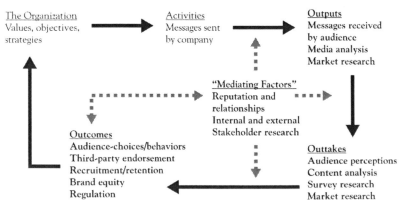

Figure 10.1. The flow of best practices.

Used with permission of *Public Relations Journal*.

to improve future programs was not gathered, then the research needs to reevaluated and redesigned to ensure these goals are met.

- *Was the return on investment for conducting the research program greater than the actual cost of the research itself?*

  Even if the research is effective in improving program performance, the cost of the research still needs to be considered. Research that costs $10,000 but only offers an incremental performance of $1,000 is a poor investment. This does not mean that research should not be conducted in this situation. Instead, the research design and the research objectives need to be reevaluated.

Applicable to a Broad Range of Activities

While the direct intent of public relations measurement and evaluation is to improve communications performance, it is essential to note that public relations does not operate in a vacuum and is typically integrated with other aspects of an organization. These need to be taken into consideration so that the benefits of the research can be used as widely as possible.

- *Is the information gathered applicable to other areas?*

  These areas can include new product development, corporate reputation, other marketing communications methods, as well as promotional use.

The Benefits of Best Practices in Public Relations Research

The benefits of best practices go beyond merely "doing it right." Following these practices offers specific business advantages. These advantages stem from generating highly reliable results that go beyond merely providing information. They are results that are actionable, improve decision making based the availability of highly reliable data, and yield a potential database that allows a comparison of findings from case to case that can also be applied to parallel communication programs. Just as important is the increase in overall quality that will lead to consistency in the application of research and the findings from that research.

Implementing Best Practices

The primary best practice that needs to be followed is the inclusion of research, measurement, and evaluation as a *core part* of a public relations program. Ideally an individual in each organization should be charged with managing this process—to know the best practices and to ensure that these best practices are followed. While there is no "standard" approach for how public relations research should be conducted, following best practices yield reliable and usable results. By following these basic guidelines, research will provide the requisite insights for improved planning, effectiveness, and demonstration of the importance and value of strategically linked communications to organizational success.

APPENDIX

Dictionary of Public Relations Measurement and Research

**This booklet was prepared and edited by
Dr. Don W. Stacks, University of Miami.**

Commission on Public Relations Measurement &
Evaluation Dictionary Editorial Board

Foreword to 2007 Edition

In the more than three years since *Dictionary of Public Relations Measurement and Research* was first released, it has become one of the most popular papers the Institute for Public Relations has ever published. Week after week, visitors to our free website (www. instituteforpr.org) download the dictionary. It has been reprinted with permission, distributed, and sometimes debated at major professional and academic conferences.

The truth is that public relations teachers and practitioners traditionally have not used the same nomenclature—let alone definitions—for many central concepts of research and measurement. Increasingly, however, it is clear that we should save our creativity for program development and execution, not for the names and meanings applied to key elements of the science beneath the art of public relations.

To that end, this second edition covers an expanded number of terms, with input from a broader group of scholars and research experts. They now represent many more countries where public relations science is regularly used. The Institute owes an enormous debt of gratitude to all of them, but particularly to Dr. Don W. Stacks. His tireless commitment to the Institute's mission is surpassed only by his commitment to family and students—and we are so very grateful to be number three on that list.

So, is the dictionary done yet? For now, maybe. But this new edition will undoubtedly receive even wider distribution, leading to even more debate, and ultimately to further evolution in our thinking about public relations research and measurement. You are invited to take part.

Frank Ovaitt
President & CEO
Institute for Public Relations

Gainesville, Florida
January 2006

Foreword to 2002 Edition

Words . . . are innocent, neutral, precise, standing for this, describing that, meaning the other . . . so if you look after them you can build bridges across incomprehension and chaos.

I don't think writers are sacred, but words are. The deserve respect. If you get the right ones in the right order they can nudge the world a little. . . .

—Tom Stoppard, *The Real Thing*

Why a dictionary for public relations measurement and research?

Because we don't all measure the same things, measure the same ways, or use the same tools or terminology. To get all of us on the same page we need to know precisely what we mean when we use or say certain words in measuring our activities and our research.

Some may complain that the words we have chosen to define are too simplistic. Remember Webster once defended his word choice by explaining that it's the little words we think we know the meaning of—but don't—which cause most of the problems in understanding and communications.

We thank Dr. Don Stacks and others who have given so generously of their time to assemble this special choice of words and politely debate each definition. We have listed their names for you and they will tell you they gratefully acknowledge that this is a work in progress. Public relations continuously evolves so there are no "final words."

> Jack Felton
> President & CEO
> Institute for Public Relations

Gainesville, Florida
September 2002

Preface to 2007 Edition

Public relations measurement and research has progressed far in the five years between the first and second editions of the Dictionary of Public Relations Measurement and Research. In its desire to answer concerns—among its own membership and from "internal" and "external" clients—about demonstrating its effectiveness, the profession began to focus on demonstrating its impact on the client's outcomes of interest. This in turn has lead to a more education in research design and evaluation methods.

The second edition of the Dictionary clearly reflects this trend. It does so in several ways. First, the Dictionary has been expanded by almost 100 terms. Second, its cross-referencing is more complete. Third, individual terms have been further designated as statistical "s" or methodological "m" within the individual term definitions. Finally, terms have been redefined and in many instances are more sophisticated—reflecting a sophistication of the profession.

I am indebted to the Commission for Public Relations Measurement and Evaluation members who toiled tirelessly to find suitable new terms and define them so that the user might better understand not only the term but also its usage(s) in the research and evaluation process. The second edition would not have been possible without their help.

I would like to acknowledge the help of Ms. Marcia L. Watson who carefully proofed and corrected versions of the second edition. She did this in addition to her other duties as a doctoral student at the University of Miami.

Finally, I would like to acknowledge the University of Miami School of Communication and Dean Sam Grogg for allowing me the time to work on this project.

Don W. Stacks
Coral Gables, Florida

Dictionary of Public Relations
Measurement and Research

– A –

Algorithm—*s.* a step-by-step problem-solving procedure, especially an established, recursive computational procedure for solving a problem in a finite number of steps

Alpha Level (α)—*s.* the amount of error or chance allowed in sampling or inferential testing

Analysis of Variance (ANOVA)—*s.* an inferential statistical test of significance for continuous measurement dependent variables against a number of groups as independent variables

Articles—*m.* an output, typically printed but also found on the Internet

Attitude—*m.* a predisposition to act or behave toward some object; a motivating factor in public relations; composed of three dimensions: affective (emotional evaluation), cognitive (knowledge evaluation), and connotative (behavioral evaluation)

Attitude Research—*m.* the measuring and interpreting a full range of views, sentiments, feelings, opinions, and beliefs that segments of the public may hold toward a client or product

Attitude Scale—*m.* a measure that targets respondent attitudes or beliefs toward some object; typically interval-level data and requires that an arbitrary or absolute midpoint ("neutral" or "neither agree nor disagree") be provided to the respondent; also known as Likert-type or Semantic Differential measures; *s.* an output measured as an interval or ratio measure

Audience—*m.* a specified group from within a defined public targeted for influence

– B –

Bar Graph—*s.* a representation of a frequency distribution by means of rectangles (or other indicators) whose widths represent class intervals and whose heights represent corresponding frequencies; *see also* graph

Baseline—*s.* an initial measurement against which all subsequent measures are compared; *m.* a data point established for comparison at the developmental stage of a research campaign.

Behavioral Event Interview (BEI)—*m.* an interview technique used to solicit evidence or examples of a specific competency or skill you possess; BEI is based on the premise that a person's past behavior is the best predictor of their future performance

Behavioral Objective—*m.* an objective that specifies the expected public relations campaign or program outcomes in terms of specific behaviors; *s.* a measure that is actionable in that it *is* the behavior requested (e.g., outcome) of a target audience; *see also* outcome

Belief—*m.* a long-held evaluation of some object, usually determined on the basis of its occurrence; clusters of beliefs yield attitudes

Benchmarking (Benchmark Study)—*m.* a measurement technique that involves having an organization learn something about its own practices, the practices of selected others, and then compares these practices

Bivariate Analysis—*s.* a statistical examination of the relationship between two variables

BRAD (British Rate and Data Measure)—*s.* British Rate and Data measure—provides circulation and advertising costs data

– C –

Campaign (Program)—*m.* the planning, execution, and evaluation of a public relations plan of action aimed at solving a problem

Case Study Methodology—*m.* an informal research methodology that gathers data on a specific individual or company or product with the analysis focused on understanding its unique qualities; is not generalizable to other cases or populations

Categorical Data—*s.* measurement data that are defined by their association with groups and are expressed in terms of frequencies, percentages, and proportions; *see also* nominal data, ordinal data

Category—*m.* in content analysis the part of the system where the content (units of analysis) are placed; also referred to as "subjects" or "buckets"

Causal Relationship—*m.* a relationship between variables in which a change in one variable forces, produces, or brings about a change in another variable; *s.* the result of a significant interaction term in an analysis of variance or regression, often displayed in path analyses or sequential equation models

Census—*m.* collection of data from *every* person or object in a population

Central Tendency—*s.* a statistic that describes the typical or average case in the distribution of a variable; *see also* mean, median, mode, range, standard deviation, standardized score, variance, Z-score

Characters—*m.* a manifest unit of analysis used in content analysis consisting of individuals or roles (e.g., occupations, roles, race)

Chi-Square (χ^2)—*s.* an inferential statistical test of significance for categorical data (nominal or ordinal)

Circulation—*s.* number of copies of a publication as distributed (as opposed to read)

Closed-Ended Question—*m.* a question that requires participants to answer selected and predetermined responses (e.g., strongly agree, agree, neither agree nor disagree, disagree, strongly disagree)

Cluster Analysis—*s.* an exploratory data analysis tool which aims at sorting different objects into groups in a way that the degree of association between two objects is maximal if they belong to the same group and minimal if otherwise

Clustered Sample—*m.* a type of probability sample that involves first breaking the population into heterogeneous subsets (or clusters), and then selecting the potential sample at random from the individual clusters

Coefficient Alpha (α)—*s.* a statistical test for a measurement's reliability for interval and ratio data; also known as Cronbach's coefficient alpha

Cohen's Kappa—*s.* an intercoder reliability measure used in content analysis when there are more than two coders; *see also* reliability, content analysis

Cohort Survey—*m.* a type of longitudinal survey in which some specific group is studied over time according to some criteria that stays the same (e.g., age = 21) while the samples may differ

Column Inches—*s.* total length of an article if it were all one-column measured in inches (or centimeters); determines the total "share of ink" that a company or brand has achieved

Communication—*m.* the process that deals with the transmission and reception of intentional messages that are a part of a natural language system (e.g., words, phrases, sentences, paragraphs)

Communication Product—*m.* the end result of the communication product process resulting in the production and dissemination of a brochure, media release, video news release, website, speech, and so forth; *see also* output, outtake

Communication(s) Audit—*m.* a systematic review and analysis of how effectively an organization communicates with all of its major internal and external audiences by identifying these audiences, by identifying the communication programs and their communication products utilized for each audience, by determining the effectiveness of these programs and their products, and by identifying gaps in the overall existing communication program; uses accepted research techniques and methodologies; *see also* formal methodology, informal methodology, case study, content analysis, survey, in-depth interview, focus group, experiment, secondary, historical, participant-observation

Communication(s) Research—*m.* any systematic study of the relationships and patterns that are developed when people seek to share information with each other

Community Case Study—*m.* an informal methodology whereby the researcher takes an in-depth look at one or several communities—subsections of communities—in which an organization has an interest by impartial, trained researchers using a mix of informal research methodologies (i.e., participant-observation, role-playing, secondary analysis, content analysis, interviewing, focus groups)

Concurrent Validity—*m.* a measurement device's ability to vary directly with a measure of the same construct or indirectly with a measure of an opposite construct. It allows you to show that your test is valid by comparing it with an already valid test

Confidence Interval—*s.* in survey methodology based on a random sampling technique, the range of values or measurement within which a population parameter is estimated to fall (e.g., for a large population

we might expect answers to a question to be within ±3% of the true
population answer; if 55% responded positively, the confidence interval would be from 52% to 58%); sometimes called measurement error

Confidence Level—*m.* in survey methodology based on a random sampling technique, the amount of confidence we can place on our confidence interval (typically set at 95%, or 95 out of 100 cases truly
representing the population under study, with *no more than* 5 cases
out of 100 misrepresenting that population); sometimes called sampling error; *s.* the amount of confidence a researcher has that a finding
between groups or categories is statistically significant; *see also* statistically significant

Construct Validity—*m.* a dimension of measurement; *s.* a statistically
tested form of measurement validity that seeks to establish the dimensionality of a measure; *see also* validity, face validity, criterion-related
validity, content validity, discriminant validity, divergent validity

Content Analysis—*m.* an informal research methodology (and measurement tool) that systematically tracks messages (written, spoken,
broadcast) and translates them into quantifiable form via a systematic approach to defining message categories through specified units
of analysis; the action of breaking down message content into predetermined components (categories) to form a judgment capable of
being measured

Content Validity—*m.* a form of measurement validity that is based on
other researchers or experts evaluations of the measurement items
contained in a measure; *see also* validity, face validity, construct validity, criterion-related validity, discriminant validity, divergent validity

Contingency Question—*m.* a survey question that is to be asked only to
some respondents, determined by their responses to some other questions; sometimes called a "funnel question"

Contingency Table—*s.* a statistical table for displaying the relationship
between variables in terms of frequencies and percentages; sometimes
called a "cross tabulation table" or "cross tab"

Continuous Data—*s.* data that are measured on a continuum, usually
as interval data

Contour Plot—*s.* a graphical technique for representing a 3-dimen-
sional surface by plotting constant z slices, called contours, on a

2-dimensional format—that is, given a value for z, lines are drawn for connecting the (x,y) coordinates where that z value occurs; used to answer the question "How does Z change as a function of X and Y?"

Convenience Sample—*m.* a nonprobability sample where the respondents or objects are chosen because of availability (e.g., "man on the street"); a type of nonprobability sample in which whoever happens to be available at a given point in time is included in the sample; sometimes called a "haphazard" or "accidental" sample

Convergent Validity—*s.* a type of construct validity that refers to the principle that the indicators for a given construct should be at least moderately correlated among themselves; *see also* coefficient alpha, validity, face validity, content validity, construct-related validity, criterion-related validity, discriminant validity, divergent validity

Correlation (r)—*s.* a statistical test that examines the relationships between variables (may be either categorical or continuous); *see also* correlation coefficient, Pearson product-moment coefficient, Spearman's rho, r

Correlation Coefficient—*s.* a measure of association that describes the direction and strength of a linear relationship between two variables; usually measured at the interval or ratio data level (e.g., Pearson Product Moment Coefficient, r), but can be measured at the nominal or ordinal level (e.g., Spearman's rho)

Cost-Effectiveness—*s.* an outcome that may be measured in public relations research that evaluates the relation between overall expenditure (costs) and results produced, usually the ratio of changes in costs to change in effects

Cost Per Thousand (CPM)—*s.* cost of advertising for each 1,000 homes reached by the media

Covariation—*s.* a criterion for causation whereby the dependent variable takes on different values depending on the independent variable

Criterion-Related Validity—*m.* a form of validity that compares one measure against others known to have specified relationships with what is being measured; the highest form of measurement validity; *see also* validity, face validity, content validity, discriminant validity, divergent validity

Criterion Variable—*m.* the variable the researchers predict to; *see also* dependent variable

Crossbreak Analysis—*s.* a categorical analysis that compares the frequency of responses in individual cells from one variable against another; *see also* crosstabulation, frequency, frequency table

Cross-Sectional Survey—*m.* a survey based on observations representing a single point in time; *see also* snapshot survey

Crosstabs—*s.* statistical tables used to array the data; allows the analyst to go beyond total data into frequencies and averages as well as to make possible overall as well as subgroup analyses (e.g., comparisons of the opinions expressed by sell-side analysts with those stated by buy-side investment professionals)

Crosstabulation—*s.* the result of two categorical variables in a table; *see also* crossbreak analysis, frequency, frequency table

Cumulative Scale (Guttman Scale/Scalogram)—*m.* a measurement scale that assumes that when you agree with a scale item you will also agree with items that are less extreme; *see also* outcome, Guttman scale, Likert scale, semantic differential scale

Cyber Image Analysis—*m.* the measurement of Internet content via chat rooms or discussion groups in cyberspace regarding a client or product or topic; the measurement of a client's image everywhere on the Internet

– D –

Data—*m.* the observations or measurements taken when evaluating a public relations campaign or program; *s.* the frequencies, means, percentages used to assess a campaign or program; *see also* nominal data, ordinal data, interval data, ratio data

Database Mining—*m.* a research technique utilizing existing data; *see also* secondary methodology

Database—*s.* a collection of data arranged for ease and speed of search and retrieval

Deduction—*m.* a philosophical logic in which specific expectations or hypotheses are developed or derived on the basis of general principles

Delphi Technique—*m.* a research methodology (usually survey or interview) where the researcher tries to forecast the future based on successive waves of interviews or surveys with a panel of experts in a given field as a means of building a "consensus" of expert opinion and thought relating to particular topics or issues

Demographic Analysis—*m.* analysis of a population in terms of special social, political, economic, and geographic subgroups (e.g., age, sex, income level, race, educational-level, place of residence, occupation)

Demographic Data—*m.* data that differentiate between groups of people or things (e.g., sex, race, income)

Dependent Variable—*m.* the variable that is measured or collected

Depth Interview—*m.* an extensive, probing, open-ended, largely unstructured interview, usually conducted in person or by telephone, in which respondents are encouraged to talk freely and in great detail about given subjects; also known as an "in-depth interview"; *see also* in-depth interview methodology

Descriptive Research—*m.* a form of research that gathers information in such a way as to paint a picture of what people think or do

Descriptive Statistics—*s.* the reduction and simplification of the numbers representing research to ease interpreting the results

Descriptive Survey—*m.* a type of survey that collects in quantitative form basic opinions or facts about a specified population or sample; also known as a "public opinion poll"

Design Bias—*m.* research design bias is introduced when the study fails to identify the validity problems or when publicity about the research fails to incorporate the researcher's cautions

Discriminant Validity—*s.* a type of validity that is determined by hypothesizing and examining differential relations between a test and measures of similar or different constructs. It is the opposite of convergent validity and is also known as divergent validity; *see also* convergent validity, divergent validity; *m.* a way of establishing if a measure is measuring what it is supposed to measure; *see also* validity, criterion-related validity

Divergent Validity—*s.* *see also* discriminant validity

Double-Barreled Question—*m.* a question that attempts to measure two things at the same time; a source of measurement error

– E –

Editorial—*m*. the content of a publication written by a journalist, as distinct from advertising content, which is determined by an advertiser; an article expressing the editorial policy of a publication of a matter of interest (also known as a "leader" or "leading article"); space in a publication bought by an advertiser that includes journalistic copy intended to make the reader think it originates from an independent source (also known as an "advertorial"); *s*. an outcome or measured variable

Environmental Scanning—*m*. a research technique for tracking new developments in any area or field by carrying out a systematic review of what appears in professional, trade, or government publications

Equal Appearing Interval Scale—*m*. a measurement scale with predefined values associated with each statement

Equivalent Advertising Value (AVE)—*s*. equivalent cost of buying space devoted to editorial content

Error Bar—*s*. a graphical data analysis technique for showing the error in the dependent variable and optionally; the independent variable in a standard x-y plot

Ethnographic Research—*m*. an informal research methodology that relies on the tools and techniques of cultural anthropologists and sociologists to obtain a better understanding of how individuals and groups function in their natural settings; *see also* participant-observation

Evaluation Research—*m*. a form of research that determines the relative effectiveness of a public relations campaign or program by measuring program outcomes (changes in the levels of awareness, understanding, attitudes, opinions, and/or behaviors of a targeted audience or public) against a predetermined set of objectives that initially established the level or degree of change desired

Events—*s*. a community affairs or sponsorship output

Experimental Methodology—*m*. a formal research methodology that imposes *strict* artificial limits or boundaries on the research in order to establish some causal relationship between variables of interest; is not generalizable to a larger population

Explanatory Research—*m*. a form of research that seeks to explain why people say, think, feel, and act the way they do; concerned primarily with the development of public relations theory about relationships and processes; are typically deductive

Exploratory Research—*m.* a form of research that seeks to establish basic attitudes, opinions, and behavior patterns or facts about a specific population or sample; are typically inductive and involve extensive probing of the population or sample or data

– F –

Face Validity—*m.* a form of measurement validity that is based on the researcher's knowledge of the concept being measured; the lowest form of measurement validity; *see also* validity, content validity, construct validity, criterion-related validity, discriminant validity, divergent validity

Facilitator—*m.* an individual who leads a focus group; also known as a moderator

Factor Analysis—*s.* a statistical tool that allows researchers to test the dimensionality of their measures; used to assess a measure's construct validity

Fever Graph—*s.* a form of line graph that measures peaks and valleys of data along a continuum that is either continuous or whose classes represent categories; *see also* graph

Field Study Methodology—*m.* a formal research methodology that imposes fewer restrictions or limits or boundaries on the research in order to test some causal relationships found in experimental research and generalize them to a larger population

Filter Question—*m.* a question that is used to move a respondent from one question to another; a question that is used to remove a respondent from a survey or interview; *see also* funnel question

Focus Group Methodology—*m.* an informal research methodology that uses a group approach to gain an in-depth understanding of a client, object, or product; is not generalizable to other focus groups or populations

Formal Methodology—*m.* a set of research methodologies that allows the researcher to generalize to a larger audience but often fails to gain in-depth understanding of the client, object, or product; a set of methodologies that follow scientific or social scientific method; a set of methodologies that are deductive in nature

Formative Evaluation—*m.* a method of evaluating the process by which programs occur while activities are in their early stages with the intent of improving or correcting activities

Frequency—*s.* a descriptive statistic that represents the number of objects being counted (e.g., number of advertisements, number of people who attend an event, number of media release pickups)

Frequency Table—*s.* a listing of counts and percentages in tabular form; may report a single variable or multiple variables; *see also* crossbreak analysis, crosstabulation

F-Test—*s.* an inferential test of significance associated with Analysis of Variance (ANOVA); *see also* Analysis of Variance

Funnel Question—*m.* a question used in a questionnaire or schedule that moves an interviewer or respondent from one part of a survey to another (e.g., "Are you a registered voter?" If the respondent says yes, certain questions are asked and if not, then other questions are asked); *see also* filter question

– G –

Goal (Objective)—*m.* the explicit statement of intentions that supports a communication strategy and includes an intended audience/receiver, a proposed measurable outcome (or desired level of change in that audience), and a specific timeframe for that change to occur

Grand Mean—*s.* a descriptive statistics which represents the mean of all sample means in a study, weighted by the number of items in each sample. The grand mean treats the individuals in the different subsets (groups) as if there were no subgroups, but only individual measures in the set. The grand mean is thus simply the mean of all of the scores; *see also* mean

Graph—*s.* a graphical representation of a variable; *see also* bar, pie, line, fever

Gross Rating Points (GRP)—*s.* measures of weight or readership or audience equivalent to audience exposure among one percent of the population; *see also* targeted gross rating points (TGRP)

Guttman Scale (Cumulative Scale/Scalogram)—*m*. a measurement scale that assumes unidimensionality and that people, when faced with a choice, will also choose items less intense than the one chosen

– H –

Histogram—*s*. a representation of a frequency distribution by means of rectangles whose widths represent class intervals and whose heights represent corresponding frequencies; a bar chart representing a frequency distribution; heights of the bars represent observed frequencies; *see also* graph

Historical Methodology—*m*. an informal research methodology that examines the causes and effects of past events

Holsti's Reliability Coefficient—*s*. a fairly simple reliability measure used in content analysis; *see also* reliability, content analysis, intercoder reliability, intracoder reliability, Scott's pi, and Krippendorf's alpha

Hypothesis—*m*. an expectation about the nature of things derived from theory; a prediction of how an independent variable changes a dependent variable; formally stated as a predication (e.g., males will purchase more of X than females), but tested via the null hypothesis (e.g., males and females will not differ in their purchases of X)

Hypothesis Testing—*m*. determining whether the expectations that a hypothesis represents are, indeed, found in the real world

– I –

Image Research—*m*. a research program or campaign that systematically studies people's perceptions toward an organization, individual, product, or service; sometimes referred to as a "reputation study"

Impressions—*m*. the number of people who might have had the opportunity to be exposed to a story that has appeared in the media; also known as "opportunity to see" (OTS); *s*. usually refers to the total audited circulation of a publication or the audience reach of a broadcast vehicle

Incidence—*s*. the frequency with which a condition or event occurs in a given time and population or sample

Independent t-Test—*s.* an inferential statistical test of significance that compares two levels of an independent variable against a continuous measured dependent variable

Independent Variable—*m.* the variable against which the dependent variable is tested

In-Depth Interview Methodology—*m.* an informal research methodology in which an individual interviews another in a one-on-one situation

Induction—*m.* a philosophical logic in which general principles are developed from specific observations

Inferential Research—*m.* statistical analyses that test if the results observed for a sample are indicative of the population; the presentation of information that allows us to make judgments whether the research results observed in a sample generalize to the population from which the sample was drawn

Inferential Statistics—*s.* statistical tests that allow a researcher to say within a certain degree of confidence whether variables or groups truly differ in their response to a public relations message; *see* analysis of variance, chi-square, bivariate correlation, correlation, Pearson product moment correlation, Spearman's rho, regression, path analysis, sequential equation model, t-test

Informal Methodology—*m.* a research methodology that does not allow the researcher to generalize to a larger audience but gains in-depth understanding of the client, object, or product

Informational Objective—*m.* an objective that establishes what information a target audience should know or the degree of change in knowledge levels after the conclusion of a public relations campaign or program

Inputs—*m.* the research information and data from both internal and external sources applied in the conception, approval, and design phases of the input stage of the communication production process

Inquiry Research—*m.* a formal or informal research methodology that employs systematically content analysis, survey methodology, and/or interviewing techniques to study the range and types of unsolicited inquiries that an organization may receive from customers, prospective customers, or other target audience groups

Instrumental Error—*m.* in measurement, error that occurs because the measuring instrument was poorly written; *s.* tested for via reliability analyses; *see also* coefficient alpha, KR-20

Intercoder Reliability—*m.* the reliability of content analysis coding when the coding is done by two or more coders; *see also* reliability, intracoder reliability, Holsti's Reliability Coefficient, Scott's pi, Krippendorf's alpha, Cohen's kappa

Interval Data—*m.* measurement data that are defined on a continuum and assumed to have equal spacing between data points; *s.* includes temperature scale, standardized intelligence test scores, Likert scale, semantic differential scale, Guttman Scalogram; *see also* attitude research, attitude scale, data, Likert scale, Guttman scale

Interview Schedule—*m.* a guideline for asking questions in person or over the telephone interviewers are tasked with predicting your likelihood of success in a given position and use your past behavior as one indicator of your future performance

Intracoder reliability—*m.* the reliability of content analysis coding when the coding is done by only one coder, usually the researcher; *s.* obtained from statistical tests that analyze coder decisions versus chance; *see also* reliability, intercoder reliability, Cohen's kappa, Holsti's reliability coefficient, Krippendorf's alpha, Scott's pi

Issues Research—*m.* a formal or informal research methodology that systematically studies public policy questions of the day, with the chief focus on those public policy matters whose definition and contending positions are still evolving

Items—*s.* a manifest unit of analysis used in content analysis consisting of an entire message itself (e.g., an advertisement, story, press release)

– J –

Judgmental Sample—*m.* a type of nonprobability sample in which individuals are deliberately selected for inclusion in the sample by the researcher because they have special knowledge, position, characteristics or represent other relevant dimensions of the population that are deemed important to study; *see also* purposive sample

– K –

Key Performance (Performance Result)—*m.* the desired end effect or impact of a program of campaign performance

Known Group t-Test—*s.* an inferential statistical test of significance that compares the results for a sampled group on some continuous measurement dependent variable against a known value; *see also* inferential statistics, independent t-test

KR-20—*s.* a reliability statistic for nominal- or ordinal-level measurement; also known as Kuder-Richardson formula 20; *see also* reliability, coefficient alpha

Krippendorf's Alpha—*s.* a fairly simple content analysis coding reliability measure; *see also* reliability, intercoder reliability, Intracoder reliability, Holsti's Reliability Coefficient, Scott's pi, Cohen's kappa

– L –

Latent Content—*m.* from content analysis, an analysis of the underlying idea, thesis, or theme of content; the deeper meanings that are intended or perceived in a message

Likert Scale—*m.* an interval-level measurement scale that requires people to respond to statements on a set of predetermined reactions, usually strongly agree, agree, neither agree nor disagree, disagree, strongly disagree; must possess an odd number of reaction words or phrases; also called "summated ratings method" because the scale requires at least two, if not three, statements per measurement dimension

Line Graph—*s.* a representation of frequency distribution by means of lines representing data points at various intervals along a continuum; *see also* graph

Longitudinal Survey—*m.* a type of survey that consists of *different* individuals or objects that is observed or measured over time (e.g., multiple snapshot samples)

– M –

Mail Survey—*m.* a survey technique whereby a questionnaire is sent to a respondent via the mail (or Internet) and the respondent self-administers the questionnaire and then sends it back

Mall Intercept Research—*m.* a special type of person-to-person surveying in which in-person interviewing is conducted by approaching prospective participants as they stroll through shopping centers or malls; a nonprobability form of sampling

Manifest Content—*m.* from content analysis, an analysis of the actual content of a message exactly as it appears as opposed to latent content that must be inferred from messages

Market Research—*m.* any systematic study of buying or selling behavior

Mean—*s.* a descriptive statistic of central tendency that describes the "average" of a set of numbers on a continuum; also called "average"; the process of applying a precise number or metric, which is both valid and reliable, to the evaluation of some performance

Measurement—*m.* a way of giving an activity a precise dimension, generally by comparison to some standard; usually done in a quantifiable or numerical manner; *see also* data, scale

Measurement Bias—*m.* failure to control for the effects of data collection and measurement (e.g. tendency of people to give socially desirable answers)

Measurement Error—*m.* the amount of error found in a research campaign; in surveys it is the amount of error in individual responses; *s.* a term that expresses the amount of doubt that a researcher may accept in terms of findings; *see also* confidence interval

Measurement Reliability—*m.* the extent to which a measurement scale measures the same thing over time; *s.* a statistical reporting of how reliable a measure is; *see also* coefficient alpha, test-retest reliability, split-half reliability

Measurement Validity—*m.* the extent to which a measurement scale actually measures what it believed to measure; *see also* face validity, content validity, construct validity, criterion-related validity

Media—*m.* includes newspapers, business and consumer magazines and other publications, radio and television, the Internet; company reports, news wires, government reports and brochures; Internet websites and discussion groups

Media Evaluations—*m.* the systematic appraisal of a company's reputation, products or services, or those of its competitors, as measured by their presence in the media

Median—*s.* a descriptive statistic of central tendency indicating the midpoint in a series of data; the point above and below which 50 percent of the data values fall

Mention Prominence—*s.* an outcome based on an indication of how prominent a company, product, or issue was mentioned in the media; typically measured in percent of article and position within the output (e.g., headline, above the fold, first three minutes)

Mentions—*s.* an output or outcome consisting of counts of incidents of a company or product or person appearing in the media, one mention constitutes a media placement

Message Content—*m.* the verbal, visual, and audio elements of a message; the material from which content analyses are conducted; *s.* a trend analysis factor that measures what, if any, of planned messages are actually contained in the media; *see also* message content analysis

Message Content Analysis—*m.* analysis of media coverage of messages regarding a client, product, or topic on key issues

Message Strength—*s.* trend analysis factor that measures how strongly a message about a client or product or topic was communicated

Mode—*s.* a descriptive statistic of central tendency indicating the most frequently occurring (the most typical) value in a data series

Moderator—*m.* an individual who leads a focus group; also known as a facilitator

Monitoring—*m.* a process by which data are systematically and regularly collected about a research program over time; *see also* environmental scanning

Motivational Objective—*m.* an objective that establishes the desired level of change in a target audience's specific attitudes or beliefs after a public relations campaign

Multiple Regression—*s.* a statistical technique that employs multiple dependent variables to predict an outcome variable (dependent variable); *see also* regression, independent variable, dependent variable

Multivariate Analysis—*s.* an inferential or descriptive statistic that examines the relationship among three or more variables

– N –

Network Analysis—*m.* a formal or informal research method that examines how individuals or units or actors relate to each other in some systematic way

Neutral Point—*s.* a point midway between extremes in attitude measurement scales; in Likert scales usually defined as "neutral" or "neither agree nor disagree"; *see also* attitude, attitude scale, Likert scale, semantic differential scale

Nominal Data—*s.* measurement data that are simple categories in which items are different in name only and do not possess any ordering; data that are mutually exhaustive and exclusive; the simplest or lowest of all data; categorical data; example: male or female, where neither is seen as better as or larger than the other

Nonparametric Statistics—*s.* inferential and descriptive statistics based on categorical data; *see also* chi-square, Spearman's rho

Non-Probability Sample—*m.* a sample drawn from a population whereby respondents or objects do not have an equal chance of being selected for observation or measurement

Nonverbal Communication—*m.* that aspect of the communication that deals with the transmission and reception of messages that are **not** a part of a natural language system (e.g., visual, spoken [as opposed to verbal], environmental)

Norm—*s.* short for "normative data"; *see also* normative data

Normal Curve—*s.* measurement data reflecting the hypothetical distribution of data points or cases based on interval-or ratio-level data that are "normally distributed" and error free; all continuous or parametric data sets have their own normally distributed data that fall under its specific normal curve

Normative Data—*s.* the proprietary set of scores that allow comparison of results to other studies and see "where you stand" and provide a context

Null Hypothesis—*s*. the hypothesis of no difference that is formally tested in a research campaign or program; its rejection is the test of the theory; it is the formal hypothesis that all inferential statistics test; *see also* inferential statistics

– O –

Objective—*m*. a measurable outcome in three forms: informational (cognitive), motivational (attitudinal/belief), behavioral (actionable); an explicit statement of intentions that supports a communication strategy, and to be measurable, includes an intended audience/public, a proposed change in a communication effect, a precise indication of the amount or level of change and a specific time frame for the change to occur

Omnibus Survey—*m*. an "all-purpose" national consumer poll usually conducted on a regular schedule (once a week or every other week) by major market research firms; also called "piggyback" or "shared-cost" survey

Open-Ended Question—*m*. open-ended questions probe the dimensions of attitudes and behavior held by a particular respondent through an interactive conversation between respondent and interviewer

Opinion—*m*. a verbalized or written evaluation of some object

Opportunities to See (OTS)—*m*. the number of times a particular audience has the potential to view a message, subject, or issue; *s*. an outcome statistic based on outputs serving as a dependent variable in some research; *see also* dependent variable, impressions, outcomes, output

Ordinal Data—*s*. measurement data that are categories in which items are different in name and possess an ordering of some sort; data that are mutually exhaustive and exclusive and ordered; categorical data; example: income as categories of under $25K, $26K–$50K, $51K–$75K, $76K–$100K, over $100K

Outcomes—*m*. quantifiable changes in awareness, knowledge, attitude, opinion, and behavior levels that occur as a result of a public relations program or campaign; an effect, consequence, or impact of a set or program of communication activities or products, and may be either short term (immediate) or long term; *s.* the dependent variable in research; *see also* dependent variable

Outgrowth—*m.* the culminating effect of all communication programs and products on the positioning of an organization in the minds of its stakeholders or publics; *s.* an outcome statistic used as a dependent variable in some research; *see also* dependent variable, outcomes

Output—*m.* what is generated as a result of a PR program or campaign that impacts on a target audience or public to act or behave in some way—this is deemed important to the researcher (also known as a "judgmental sample"); the final stage of a communication product, production, or process resulting in the production and dissemination of a communication product (brochure, media release, website, speech, etc.); *s.* the number of communication products or services resulting from a communication production process; the number distributed and/or the number reaching a targeted audience; sometimes used as an outcome serving as a dependent variable in research; *see also* dependent variable, outcome

Outtake—*m.* measurement of what audiences have understood and/ or heeded and/or responded to a communication product's call to seek further information from PR messages prior to measuring an outcome; audience reaction to the receipt of a communication product, including favorability of the product, recall and retention of the message embedded in the product, and whether the audience heeded or responded to a call for information or action within the message; *s.* sometimes used as an outcome serving as a dependent variable in research; *see also* dependent variable, outcome

– P –

Paired t-Test—*s.* an inferential statistical test of significance that compares data that are collected twice on the same sample; *see also* inferential statistics, independent t-test, known-group t-test

Panel Survey—*m.* a type of survey that consists of the *same* individuals or objects that are observed or measured over time; a type of survey in which a group of individuals are deliberately recruited by a research firm because of their special demographic characteristics for the express purpose of being interviewed more than once over a period of time for various clients on a broad array of different topics or subjects

Parameter—*s.* in sampling, a characteristic of a population that is of interest

Parametric Statistics—*s.* inferential and descriptive statistics based on continuous data; *see also* data, descriptive statistics, inferential statistics

Participant-Observation—*m.* an informal research methodology where the researcher takes an active role in the life of an organization or community, observes and records interactions, and then analyzes those interactions

Path Analysis—*s.* a statistical technique that establishes relationships between variables with arrows between variables indicating the pattern of causal relationships usually in the form of a "path diagram"; *see also* path diagram

Path Diagram—*s.* a graphical representation of the causal relationships between variables showing both direction and strength of relationship

Pearson Product-Moment Coefficient (*r*)—*s.* a correlation statistic used with interval and ratio data; *see also* correlation, data, Spearman's rho

Percentage—*s.* a descriptive statistic based on categorical data; defined as the frequency count for a particular category divided by the total frequency count; example: 10 males out of 100 people = 10%; *see also* descriptive statistics

Percentage Point—*s.* the number that a percentage is increased or decreased

Percent of Change—*s.* a measure of increase or decrease of media coverage

Performance—*m.* the act of carrying out, doing, executing, or putting into effect; a deed, task, action, or activity as a unit of a program of performance

Performance Indicator—*m.* a sign or parameter that, if tracked over time, provides information about the ongoing results of a particular program of performance or campaign; *s.* an outcome measured during a public relations campaign that serves as a dependent variable; *see also* data, dependent variable

Performance Measure—*m.* a number that shows the exact extent to which a result was achieved; *s.* in a research campaign, an outcome of some sort serving as a dependent variable; *see also* data, dependent variable, outcomes

Performance Result (Key Performance)—*m*. the desired end effect or impact of a program of campaign performance

Performance Target—*m*. a time-bounded and measurable commitment toward achieving a desired result

Periodicity—*s*. a bias found in sampling due to the way in which the items or respondents are chosen; example: newspapers may differ by being daily, weekly, weekday only, and so forth

Pie Graph—*s*. a representation of a frequency distribution by means of triangular portions of a pie whose sections represents the percentages of the variable of interest; *see also* graph

Piggyback Survey—*m*. *see* omnibus survey

Poll—*m*. a form of survey research that focuses more on immediate behavior than attitudes; a very short survey-like method whose questionnaire asks only very short and closed-ended questions; *see also* indepth interview survey, survey methodology

Positioning—*m*. trend analysis factor that measures how a client or product or topic was positioned in the media (e.g., leader, follower)

Position Papers—*m*. print output

Probability Sample—*m*. a sample drawn at random from a population such that all possible respondents or objects have an equal chance of being selected for observation or measurement

Probe Question—*m*. a question used in a questionnaire or schedule that requires the participant to explain an earlier response, often in the form of "why do you think this?"

Product (Communication Product)—*m*. the end result of the communication product or process resulting in the production and dissemination of a brochure, media release, video news release, website, speech, and so forth; an output or outtake; *see also* output, outtake

Program (Campaign)—*m*. the planning, execution, and evaluation of a public relations plan of action aimed at solving a problem

Prominence of Mention—*m*. trend analysis factor that measures how prominently a client or product or topic was mentioned and where that mention occurred (e.g., headline, top of the fold, what part of a broadcast); *s.* an output unit of analysis used as a dependent variable; *see also* dependent variable, output

Proportion—*s.* a descriptive statistic based on categorical data; defined as the percentage as made part of one (1.0); example: 10 males out of 100 people are 10 hundredths of the sample

PR Return on Investment (PRROI)—*m.* the impact of a public relations program on business investment; *s.* the outcome (dependent) variable that demonstrates the impact of a public relations campaign or program investment on the overall business outcomes; a causal indicator of public relations impact; *see also* causal relationships, Return on Investment (ROI)

Psychographic Research—*m.* research focusing on a population or sample's nondemographic traits and characteristics, such as personality type, lifestyle, social roles, values, attitudes, and beliefs

Psychometrics—*s.* a branch of psychology that deals with the design, administration, and interpretation of quantitative tests for the measurement of psychological variables such as intelligence, aptitude, and personality traits; also called psychometry

Public—*m.* a group of people who have consequences for an organization or are affected by the consequences of organizational decisions; a group of people from which the public relations campaign or program selects specific targeted audiences in an attempt to influence it regarding a company, product, issue, or individual; *see also* audience, sample

Public Opinion Poll—*m.* a type of survey that collects basic opinions or facts about a specified population or sample; also known as a descriptive survey; *see also* poll, survey methodology

Public Relations Effectiveness—*s.* the degree to which the outcome of a public relations program is consonant with the overall objectives of the program as judged by some measure of causation; *see also* causal relationship.

Purposive Sample—*m.* a nonprobability sample in which individuals are deliberately selected for inclusion based on their special knowledge, position, characteristics, or relevant dimensions of the population

Push Poll—*m.* a survey technique in which an interviewer begins by acting as if the telephone call is a general survey but then asks the respondent a question implying questionable behaviors or outcomes of a person or product

– Q –

Q-Sort—*m.* a measurement instrument that focuses on respondents' beliefs by asking them to sort through piles of opinion statement and sort them into piles on an 11-point continuum usually bounded by "most-like-me" to "most-unlike-me"; *see also* attitude scale

Qualitative Research—*m.* usually refers to studies that are somewhat to totally subjective, but nevertheless in-depth, using a probing, open-ended, response format or reflects an ethnomethodological orientation

Quantitative Research—*m.* usually refers to studies that are highly objective and projectable, using closed-ended, forced-choice question-naires; research that relies heavily on statistics and numerical measures

Question—*m.* a statement or phrase used in a questionnaire or schedule that elicits either an open- or closed-ended response from a research participant; *see also* funnel questions, probe questions

Questionnaire—*m.* a measurement instrument that contains exact ques-tions and measures an interviewer or survey researcher uses to survey through the mail, Internet, in person, or via the telephone; may be closed-ended and open-ended, but typically employs more closed-ended questions

Quota Sample—*m.* a type of nonprobability sample that draws its sample based on a percentage or quota from the population and stops sam-pling when that quota is met; a nonprobability sample that *attempts* to have the same general distribution of population characteristics as in the sample; *see also* poll, survey methodology

– R –

Range—*s.* a descriptive central tendency statistic that expresses the dif-ference between the highest and lowest scores in the data set; example: responses to a question on a 1 to 5 Likert scale where all reaction cat-egories were used would yield a range of 4 (5 minus 1)

Ratio Data—*s.* measurement data that are defined on a continuum and possess an absolute zero point; examples: number of children, a bank account, absolute lack of heat (0° Kelvin = –459.67° or –273.15° C)

Reach—*m.* refers to the scope or range of distribution and thus coverage that a given communication product has in a targeted audience group; broadcasting, the net unduplicated (also called "duplicated") radio or TV audience for programs or commercials as measured for a specific time period

Readership—*m.* number of people who actually read each issue of a publication on average; *s.* an outcome variable that often serves as a dependent variable; *see also* dependent variable, outcome

Regression—*s.* a statistical tool that predicts outcomes based on one outcome (dependent) variable and one predictor (independent) variable; *see also* multiple regression; *m.* a source of error or invalidity in experimental methodology that may impact on the validity of the experiment; *see also* experimental methodology, validity, inferential statistics

Reliability—*m.* the extent to which results would be consistent, or replicable, if the research were conducted a number of times; *s.* a statistical measure accessing consistency of a measure, usually through the coefficient alpha or KR-20 statistic in measurement or Cohen's kappa, Hosti's reliability coefficient, Krippendorf's alpha, or Scott's pi; *see also* measurement reliability, Cohen's Kappa, Holsti's reliability coefficient, Scott's pi

Reputation—*s.* an outcome variable often used dependent variable in public relations research dealing with the public's perception of some source's credibility, trustworthiness, or image based on the source's behavior; *see also* dependent variable

Research Bias—*m.* unknown or unacknowledged error created during the design, measurement, sampling, procedure, or choice of problem studied; *see also* experimental methodology, validity, regression

Research Instrument—*m.* tool used to collect data; *see also* questionnaire, interview schedule, semistructured interview, structured interview

Research—*m.* the systematic effort before (formative research) or during and/or after (summative or evaluative research) a communication activity aimed at discovering and collecting the facts or opinions pertaining to an identified issue, need, or question; may be formal or informal

Respondent—*m.* the individual from whom data are collected through participation in a research campaign; sometimes called participant or, in psychological study, subject

Response Rate—*m.* from survey methodology, the number of respondents who actually completed an interview; *s.* the percentage of completed surveys (often adjusted for mailing errors)

Results—*s.* the outcome demonstrated to have been impacted upon by a public relations campaign; *m.* that which is measured in a campaign as dependent variables; *see also* dependent variable, outcome, output, outtake, outgrowth

Return on Investment (ROI)—*s.* an outcome variable that equates profit from investment; *see also* public relations effectiveness, dependent variable

– S –

Sample—*m.* a group of people or objects chosen from a larger population; *see also* probability sample, nonprobability sample; convenience sample; panel survey; longitudinal survey; snapshot survey

Sampling Error—*m.* the amount of error expected or observed in surveys that may be attributed to problems in selecting respondents; *s.* the amount of error that is acceptable or expected based on the sample size and expressed as confidence in sampling form a population; *see also* confidence level

Scale—*m.* a measurement instrument consisting of attitude or belief items that reflect an underlying structure toward some attitude or belief object; *see also* attitude scale

Scalogram (Guttman Scale/Cumulative Scale)—*m.* a measurement scale that assumes (a) unidimensionality and (b) that people, when faced with a choice, will also choose items less intense than the one chosen; *see also* attitude scale, Likert scale, semantic differential scale

Scattergram—*s.* a descriptive statistics based on continuous data that graphically demonstrated how data are distributed between two variables; also known as a scatter diagram or scatterplot

Schedule—*m.* the timeline on which a public relations program or campaign is conducted; a list of questions, usually open-ended, used in focus group and in-depth interviews to gather data; *see also* survey methodology, in-depth interview methodology

Scott's pi—*s.* a coding reliability measure employed in content analysis that reduces the impact of chance agreement among intercoder or intracoder coding; *see also* reliability, content analysis, Holsti's reliability coefficient, Krippendorf's alpha, Cohen's kappa

Screener Question—*m.* one of several questions usually asked at the beginning of an interview or survey to determine if the potential respondent is eligible to participate in the study; *see also* funnel question

Secondary Methodology—*m.* an informal research methodology that examines extant data in order to draw conclusions; a systematic reanalysis of a vast array of existing data; often used in benchmarking and benchmark studies

Semantic Differential Scale—*m.* an attitude measure that asks respondents to evaluate an attitude object based on bipolar adjectives or phrases separated by a continuum represented as consisting of an odd number of intervals; developed by Osgood, Suci, and Tannenbaum; *see also* attitude scale, Guttman scale, Likert scale

Semantic Space—*m.* the idea that people can evaluate attitude objects along some spatial continuum; often associated with attitude researchers Osgood, Suci, and Tannenbaum

Semistructured Interview—*m.* an interview conducted with a fairly open framework that allows for focused, conversational, two-way communication; it can be used both to give and receive information

Sequential Equation Model—*s.* a statistical methodology similar to path analysis but that uses as measures that are created such as attitude, intelligence, reputation rather than actual indicators (e.g., sales, revenue) to test a hypothesized causal relationship between predictor (independent) and outcome (dependent) variables; *see also* dependent variable, independent variable, path analysis, regression, multiple regression

Share of Ink (SOI)—*s.* measurement of the total press/magazine coverage found in articles or mentions devoted to a particular industry or topic as analyzed to determine what percent of outputs or Opportunities to

See (OTS) is devoted to a client or product; an outcome often used as a dependent variable; *see also* dependent variable, outcome

Share of Voice (SOV)—*s.* measurement of total coverage devoted to radio/television coverage to a particular industry or topic as analyzed to determine what percent of outputs or Opportunities to See (OTS) is devoted to a client or product; also known as "share of coverage"; an outcome often used as a dependent variable; *see also* dependent variable, outcome

Shared-Cost Survey—*m. see* omnibus survey

Simple Random Sample—*m.* a type of probability sample in which numbers are assigned to each member of a population, a random set of numbers is generated, and then only those members having the random numbers are included in the sample

Situation Analysis—*m.* an impartial, often third-party assessment of the public relations and/or public affairs problems, or opportunities, that an organization may be facing at a given point in time

Skip Interval—*m.* the distance between people selected from a population based on systematic sampling; usually defined as the total population divided by the number of people to be sampled (e.g., for a sample of 100 people to be drawn from a population of 10,000 people, the skip interval would be 100/10,000 = 100 individuals skipped between selected participants)

Snapshot Survey—*m.* a type of survey that consists of individuals or objects that is observed or measured once; *see also* cross-sectional survey

Snowball Sample—*m.* a type of nonprobability sample in which individuals who are interviewed are asked to suggest other individuals for further interviewing

Sociogram—*s.* a pictorial representation of the actual relationships of individuals within a specified unit such as a public, target audience, or work unit

Sources Mentioned—*m.* trend analysis factor that measures who was quoted in media coverage; also known as "quoteds"

Speaking Engagements—*s.* print or broadcast or Internet communication product output; *see also* output

Spearman's rho—*s.* a correlation statistic used with nominal or ordinal data; *see also* correlation, data, Pearson product-moment coefficient

Split-Half Reliability—*s.* a test for a measure's reliability where a sample is randomly split and one segment receives a part of the measure and the second segment receives the rest

Standard Deviation (SD)—*s.* a descriptive statistic of central tendency that indexes the variability of a distribution; the range from the mean within which approximately 34% of the cases fall, provided the values are distributed in a normal curve

Standardized Score (Z-Score)—*s.* a descriptive statistic based on continuous data that expresses individual scores based on their standard deviations from the group mean; range of scores is usually −3.00 to +3.00; *see also* z-score

Statistical Significance—*s.* refers to the degree to which relationships observed in a sample can be attributed to sampling error or measurement error alone; expressed in terms of confidence that the relationships are due to error X% of the time (e.g., 5%); expressed in terms of the confidence that we have that the results are due to what was measured X% of the time (e.g., 95% confident); *see also* inferential statistics, confidence interval

Stratified Sample—*m.* a type of probability sample that involves first breaking the total population into homogenous subsets (or strata) and then selecting the potential sample at random from the individual strata; example: stratifying on race would require breaking the population into racial strata and then randomly sampling within each stratum

Structured Interview—*m.* an interview with a predefined set of questions and responses that may provide more reliable, quantifiable data than an open-ended interview and can be designed rigorously to avoid biases in the line of questioning

Summary Measure—*s.* summary measures combine information of different types and from different sources, which together, permit a rapid appraisal of a specific phenomenon to identify differences (e.g. between groups, countries), observed changes over time, or expected changes (e.g. as a consequence of policy measures); there are four key elements to summary measures: the selection of relevant parameters to be included, the reliable measurement/collection of these parameters, the unit in which the summary measure will be expressed, and the relative weight of each of the constituents in the total summary measure

Summative Evaluation—*m.* a method of evaluating the end of a research program; the basis of establishing the dependent measures; *see also* dependent variable

Survey Methodology—*m.* a formal research methodology that seeks to gather data and analyze a population's or sample's attitudes, beliefs, and opinions; data are gathered in person or by telephone (face-to-face), or self-administered via mail, e-mail, or fax; *see also* survey methodology, longitudinal survey, panel survey, cohort survey, snapshot survey

Symbols/Words—*s.* a manifest unit of analysis used in content analysis consisting of specific words (e.g., pronouns, client name, logotypes) that are counted; *see also* content analysis

Systematic Sample—*m.* a type of probability sample in which units in a population are selected from an available list at a fixed interval after a random start

– T –

Target Audience—*m.* a very specific audience differentiated from "audience" by some measurable characteristic or attribute (e.g., sports fishermen)

Targeted Gross Rating Points (TGRP)—*s.* gross rating points (GRP) targeted to a particular group or target audience; an outcome often used as a dependent variable; *see also* dependent variable, gross rating points, outcome

Test-Retest Reliability—*s.* a test for a measure's reliability by testing the same sample with the same measure over time

Themes—*s.* a latent unit of analysis used in content analysis that measures an underlying theme or thesis (e.g., sexuality, violence, credibility); *see also* content analysis

Throughputs—*m.* the development, creative, and production activities (writing, editing, creative design, printing, fabrication, etc.) as part of a throughput stage of a communication product production process

Time/Space Measures—*s.* a manifest unit of analysis used in content analysis consisting of physically measurable units (e.g., column inches, size of photographs, broadcast time for a story); *see also* content analysis

Tone—*s.* trend and latent content analysis factor that measures how a target audience feels about the client or product or topic; typically defined as positive, neutral/balanced, or negative; often used as an outcome and dependent variable; *see also* dependent variable, outcome, content analysis

Trend Analysis—*m.* tracking of performance over the course of a PR campaign or program; survey method whereby a topic or subject is examined over a period of time through repeated surveys of independently selected samples (snapshot or cross-sectional survey)

t-Test—*s.* an inferential statistical test of significance for continuous measurement dependent variables against a bivariate independent variable; used when total number of observations are less than 100; *see also* paired t-test; independent t-test; known group t-test, inferential statistics

Type of Article—*m.* categories of a publication such as "product review," "by-lined article," "editorial," "advertorial," and "feature story"; *s.* trend analysis factor that measures the nature of client or product or topic coverage (e.g., column inches, broadcast time); often used as a dependent variable; *see also* dependent variable

– U –

Unit of Analysis—*m.* the specification of what is to be counted in content analysis methodology; consist of symbols/words, time/space measures, characters, themes, and items; may be *manifest* (observable) or *latent* (attitudinal)

Univariate Analysis—*s.* the examination of only one variable at a time

Universe—*m.* the set of all the units from which a sample is drawn; also called the population

– V –

Validity—*m.* the extent to which a research project actually measures what it is intended, or purports to measure; *see also* measurement validity

Value—*m.* an underlying cultural expectation that usually directs an individual's beliefs

Variance (σ^2)—*s.* a descriptive statistic of central tendency that measures the extent to which individual scores in a data set differ from each other; the sum of the squared standard deviations from the mean

Verbatim—*m.* a transcript of the actual comments participants make in a focus group or individuals. Many researchers include verbatims in their final reports to support their interpretation of the finding; *s.* data that may be used in content analysis; *see also* interview schedule, semi-structured interview, structured interview, content analysis

– W –

Weighted Average—*s.* an average that takes into account the proportional relevance of each component rather than treating each component equally

Weighting—*s.* assigning a numerical coefficient to an item to express its relative importance in a frequency distribution

Word/Symbol—*s.* from content analysis, a unit of analysis consisting of the actual word or symbol communicated in the media; *see also* content analysis

– Z –

Z-Score (Standardized Score)—*s.* a descriptive statistic of central tendency that takes data from different types of scales and standardizes them as areas under the normal curve for comparison purposes; *see also* standardized score

The Commission on Public Relations Measurement & Evaluation

Formed under the auspices of the Institute for Public Relations, the Commission exists to establish standards and methods for public relations research and measurement, and to issue authoritative best-practices white papers.

The Institute for Public Relations

This independent foundation is dedicated to the science beneath the art of public relations. The Institute exists to build and document research-based knowledge in the field of public relations, and to mainstream this knowledge by making it available and useful to practitioners, educators, researchers, and the clients they serve.

A wide array of papers authored by members of the Commission on Public Relations Measurement & Evaluation can be found at www.instituteforpr.org.

Notes

Chapter 1

1. Grunig and Hunt (1984).
2. Stacks (2010).
3. Wright (1990).
4. Stacks (2010).
5. *New York Times*, September 11, 1990, pp. D21.
6. Group Attitudes Corporation was founded by John and Jane Mapes in 1950 and acquired by Hill & Knowlton in 1956; *New York Times* (September 11, 1990).
7. Legacy Tobacco Documents Library, University of California, San Francisco.
8. See Miller and Burgoon (1974); Miller and Levine (2009).
9. International Association for Measurement and Evaluation of Communication formerly known as the Association of Media Evaluation Companies (AMEC); www.amecorg.com.
10. The Commission on Public Relations Research and Evaluation and the Research Fellows are affiliated with the Institute for Public Relations (www.instituteforpr.org).
11. This includes only companies headquartered in the United States and United Kingdom. Other companies specializing in this area operate in other regions of the world.
12. Dozier, Grunig, and Grunig (1995); Grunig (1992); Grunig, Grunig, and Dozier (2002); Grunig and Hunt (1984); Toth (2009).
13. Broom and Dozier (1990).
14. Taylor (1919).
15. Michaelson and Macleod (2007).
16. PricewaterhouseCoopers, "Global Best Practices," http://www.pwc.com
17. Bowen, Rawlins, and Martin (2010).

Chapter 2

1. For more on integrated marketing communication (IMC), see Caywood (1997); Harris (1993); Harris (1998); Schutz, Tannenbaum, and Lauterborn (1998).
2. Arthur W. Page Society (2009); see also Bowen, Rawlins, and Martin (2010).
3. Wright (1990).
4. Wright (1990).

5. Stacks (2007), p. 8.

6. Stacks (2007), p. 14.

7. Wright (1990).

8. Stacks (2010).

9. Michaelson and Griffin (2009).

10. Stacks (2010).

11. Stacks (2007).

12. Stacks (2010).

13. Stacks (2007).

14. Stacks (2007), p. 17

15. Michaelson and Stacks (2007); Stacks and Michaelson (2009), pp. 1–22.

16. Stacks (2010).

17. Weiner (2007).

18. Daniels (2009).

19. Stacks and Michaelson (2009).

20. Carroll (2006).

Chapter 3

1. For more on measurement, see Stacks and Carroll (2004). The bibliography is broken into sections and ranges from introductory to advanced reference materials from professional and academic sources.

2. Stacks (2010), chapter 3.

3. Commission on Public Relations Measurement and Evaluation (October 16, 2009).

4. See, for instance, Botan and Hazelton (2006); Stacks and Salwen (2009).

5. Stacks (2010).

6. See Stacks (2010), especially chapters 3 and 4.

7. For an historic overview, see Dillard and Pfau (2002); Likert (1932); Thurstone and Chave (1929).

8. For an excellent overview, see Dillard and Pfau (2002).

9. Miller (2002).

10. Thurstone and Chave (1929).

11. Likert (1932).

12. Osgood, Suci, and Tannenbaum (1957).

13. Stacks (2010), chapter 3.

14. Stacks (2010).

15. This is done through a statistical test called factor analysis. Although beyond the scope of this volume, factor analysis takes the items in a scale and tests to see how they are related to each other. A "factor" or "dimension" emerges from the correlations that have been "stretched" to ensure a maximum relationship and for other items that appear to be close within that dimension. There are two types of factor analysis: exploratory factor analysis (EFA), used when creating

a new measure, and confirmatory factor analysis (CFA), which analyses the factor structure of an extant measure. Regardless of whether a measure is being created or an existing measure is being used, factor analysis should be conducted on participant responses to the measure. EFA and CFA are not reliability analyses.

16. Miller (2002).

17. Rubin, Palmgreen, and Sypher (1994); Rubin, Rubin, and Haridakisk (2010).

18. Michaelson and Stacks (2007); Stacks and Michaelson (2004); Stacks and Michaelson (2009), pp. 1–22.

19. Stacks and Michaelson (2009), pp 1–22.

20. McCroskey, Richmond, and Daly (1975), pp. 323–332.

Chapter 4

1. See Jeffries (April 3, 2006); Lindenmann (2001).

2. See Brody and Stone (1989).

3. Stacks (2010), chapter 7.

4. For a general discussion of these questions see Hocking, Stacks, and McDermott (2003); see Stacks (2010) for relationships to public relations research.

5. Stacks (2007).

6. Search Engine Optimization, http://en.wikipedia.org/wiki/Search_engine_optimization

7. Stacks (2010); Stacks (2002).

8. McCormick (1985), pp. 87–96.

9. Hocking, Stacks, and McDermott (2003).

10. Case is courtesy of Echo Research LTD.

Chapter 5

1. Stacks (2006), p. 18.

2. Stacks (2006), p. 18.

3. Geertz (1976).

4. Michaelson (1979).

5. A typical scale may be "strongly agree," "somewhat agree," "neither agree nor disagree," "somewhat disagree," or "strongly disagree."

6. For a discussion, see Hocking, Stacks, and McDermott (2003).

7. Stacks (2006), p. 16.

8. Stacks (2006), p. 7.

9. It is not possible to identify the actual company, as it was bought out after a hostile takeover attempt failed and senior leadership were not allowed to release its name.

Chapter 6

1. Stacks (2010).
2. Holsti (1969).
3. Stacks (2010).
4. Holsti (1969); Scott (1955).
5. Stacks and Michaelson (2009), pp. 1–22.
6. For a more detailed discussion, see Jeffries-Fox (2003).
7. Tinsley and Weiss (2000).
8. For more discussion, see Broom and Dozier (1990); Stacks (2010).
9. Michaelson and Griffin (2009).

Chapter 7

1. Stacks (2007), p 17
2. Stacks (2007), p. 17.
3. Stacks (2007), p. 22
4. Stacks (2007), p. 16.
5. Stacks (2010).
6. Stacks (2010).
7. For more on this, see Backstrom and Hirsch-Cesar (1981).
8. The intercept is particularly useful in marketing public relations.
9. Dillman (2007).
10. Stacks (2010).
11. Stacks (2010); see especially Hickson (2003), pp. 193–215.
12. Stacks (2010).
13. For a complete analysis of public relations experimentation, see Stacks (2010), chapter 12.
14. For more on experimental design and controls, see Campbell and Stanley (1963).
15. Michaelson and Stacks (2007); Stacks and Michaelson (2009), pp. 1–22.
16. Dillman (2007).

Chapter 8

1. SPSS has been around for at least 30 years. Initially known as the "Statistical Package for the Social Sciences," it is used by many academics and professionals to compute statistics. In 2009 SPSS was purchased by IBM and in the future will be known as IBM® SPSS® Statistics.
2. For more on the actual computing, see Stacks (2010).
3. For more, see Blalock (1972); a communication-based easy read is found in Williams and Monge (2001).
4. Hocking, Stacks, and McDermott (2003).

5. This is beyond the scope of this book, but the t-test is based on a sensitive measure of variance for each mean. As a sample gets larger, the variance becomes larger and the test's ability to take that into account is reduced. For more on this, see Blalock (1972), pp. 192–193.

6. See Williams and Monge (2001), chap. 8.

7. For a fairly simple read on regression, see Allison (1999).

Chapter 9

1. U.S. Census Bureau (2009).

2. See Stacks (2010), chapters 4, 10, and 13.

3. Backstrom and Gursch-Cesar (1981).

4. Waksberg (1978), pp. 40–46.

Chapter 10

1. Sections of this chapter were initially published in Michaelson and Macleod (2007).

2. See Stacks (2010), chapter 2.

3. We can no longer get away with measuring publics; they are too heterogeneous in a global business environment that is so clearly interconnected via the Internet.

4. See Rawlins (2007).

5. For definitions of these and other terms, see Stacks (2007).

References

Allison, P. D. (1999). *Multiple regression: A primer*. Thousand Oaks, CA: Pine Forge Press.

Arthur W. Page Society. (2009). *The authentic enterprise*. New York, NY: Author. Retrieved from www.awpagesociety.com/site/members/page _society_releases_the_authentic_enterprise/

Backstrom, H., & Hirsch-Cesar, G. (1981). *Survey research* (2nd ed.). New York, NY: Macmillan.

Blalock, H. J. (1972). *Social statistics*. New York, NY: McGraw-Hill.

Botan, C., & Hazelton, V. (2006). *Public relations theory II*. Mahwah, NJ: Lawrence Erlbaum.

Bowen, S. A., Rawlins, B., & Martin, T. (2010). *An overview of the public relations function*. New York, NY: Business Expert Press.

Brody, E. W., & Stone, G. C. (1989). *Public relations research*. New York, NY: Praeger.

Broom, G. M., and Dozier, D. (1990). *Using research in public relations: Applications to program management*. Englewood Cliffs, NJ: Prentice Hall.

Campbell, D. T., & Stanley, J. C. (1963). *Experimental and quasi-experimental designs for research*. Chicago, IL: Rand McNally.

Carroll, T. B. (2006, March 9–12). *Does familiarity breed contempt? Analyses of the relationship among company familiarity, company reputation, company citizenship, and company personality on corporate equity*. Paper presented at the Ninth Annual International Public Relations Research Conference, Miami, FL.

Caywood, C. L. (Ed.). (1997). *The handbook of strategic public relations and integrated communications*. New York, NY: McGraw-Hill.

Commission on Public Relations Measurement and Evaluation. Meeting minutes, October 16, 2009.

Daniels, C. (2009, October 29). Study: Recession didn't slow consumers' appetite for cause-fueled products. *PR Week*, October 29. Retrieved from www.prweekus.com/Study-Recession-didnt-slow-consumers-appetite -for-cause-fueled-products/article/155871/

Dillard, J. P., & Pfau, M. (2002). *The persuasion handbook*. Newbury, CA: Sage.

Dillman, D. A. (2007). *Mail and Internet surveys: A tailored design method* (2nd ed.). New York, NY: Wiley.

Dozier, D., Grunig, L., & Grunig, J. E. (1995). *Manager's guide to excellence in public relations and communication management*. Hillsdale, NJ: Lawrence Erlbaum.

Echo Research. (2008). "Media Assessment of Saudi Arabia's Reputation and Foreign Perceptions."

Geertz, C. (1976). "From the native point of view": On the nature of anthropological understanding. In K. H. Basso & H. A. Selby (Eds.), *Meaning in anthropology* (pp. 221–237). Albuquerque, NM: University of New Mexico Press.

Grunig, J. E. (1992). *Excellence in public relations and communication management.* Hillsdale, NJ: Lawrence Erlbaum.

Grunig, J. E., & Hunt, T. (1984). *Managing public relations.* Orlando, FL: Harcourt Brace Jovanovich.

Grunig, L. A., Grunig, J. E., & Dozier, D. M. (2002). *Excellent public relations and effective organizations: A study of communication management in three countries.* Mahwah, NJ: Lawrence Erlbaum.

Harris, T. L. (1993). *The marketer's guide to public relations.* New York, NY: John Wiley & Sons.

Harris, T. L. (1998). *Value-added public relations: The secret weapon on integrated marketing.* Lincolnwood, IL: NTC Business Books.

Hickson, M. L. (2003). Qualitative research. In J. E. Hocking, D. W. Stacks, & S. T. McDermott, *Communication research* (3rd ed., pp. 193–215). Boston, MA: Allyn & Bacon.

Hocking, J. E., Stacks, D. W., & McDermott, S. T. (2003). *Communication research* (3rd ed.). Boston, MA: Allyn & Bacon.

Holsti, O. R. (1969). *Content analysis for the social sciences and humanities.* Reading, MA: Addison-Wesley.

International Association for Measurement and Evaluation of Communication (formerly known as the Association of Media Evaluation Companies [AMEC]); http://www.amecorg.com

Jeffries, A. (2006, April 3). Great research tips for the budget-strapped. *PR News,*.

Jeffries-Fox, B. (2003). *Advertising value equivalency.* Gainesville, FL: Institute for Public Relations. Retrieved from http://www.instituteforpr.org/ipr_info/adv_value_equiv/

Legacy Tobacco Documents Library, University of California, San Francisco. Retrieved from http://legacy.library.ucsf.edu/

Likert, R. (1932). A technique for the measurement of attitudes. *Archives of Psychology, 40,* 1–55.

Lindenmann, W. K. (2001). *Research does not have to put you in the poorhouse.* Gainesville, FL: Institute for Public Relations. Retrieved from www.instituteforpr.org/research/affordability/

McCormick, M. (1985). *The New York Times guide to reference materials* (rev. ed., pp. 87–96). New York, NY: Praeger.

McCroskey, J. C., Richmond, V. P., & Daly, J. A. (1975). The development of a measure of perceived homophily in interpersonal communication. *Human Communication Research, 1*, 323–332.

Michaelson, D. (1979). *From ethnography to ethnology: A study of the conflict of interpretations of the southern Kwakiutl potlatch.* Ann Arbor, MI: University Microforms, p. 140.

Michaelson, D., & Griffin, T. (2009). *The media reality check: A new approach to content analysis.* Gainesville, FL: Institute for Public Relations. Retrieved from www .instituteforpr.org/files/uploads/JFGRAMetLifeandEchoResearch.pdf

Michaelson, D., & Macleod, S. (2007). The application of "best practices" in public relations measurement and evaluation systems. *Public Relations Journal, 1*, 1–14. Retrieved from www.prsa.org/prjournal/fall07.html

Michaelson, D., & Stacks D. W. (2007). *Exploring the comparative communications effectiveness of advertising and media placement.* Gainesville, FL: Institute for Public Relations. Retrieved from http://www.instituteforpr.org/research_single/ exploring_the_comparative_communications/

Miller, D. (2002). *Handbook of research design and social measurement* (6th ed.). Newbury Park, CA: Sage.

Miller, G. R., & Burgoon, M. (1974). *New techniques of persuasion.* New York, NY: Holt, Rinehart & Winston.

Miller, M. D., & Levine, T. (2009). Persuasion. In D. W. Stacks and M. B. Salwen (Eds.), *An integrated approach to communication theory and research* (2nd ed., pp. 245–259). New York, NY: Routledge.

Osgood, C., Suci, G., & Tannenbaum, P. (1957). *The measurement of meaning.* Urbana, IL: University of Illinois Press.

PricewaterhouseCoopers. (2009). *Global best practices.* Retrieved from www.globalbestpractices.com/Home/Document.aspx?Link=Best+practices/ FAQs&Idx=BestPracticesIdx.

Rawlins, B. (2007). *Corporate and governmental transparency (openness).* Paper presented at the International Congress on Corporate Communication, Barranquilla, Colombia, September 6–7.

Rubin, R. B., Palmgreen, P., & Sypher, H. E. (1994). *Communication research measures: A sourcebook.* New York, NY: Guilford.

Rubin, R. B., Rubin, A., & Haridakisk, H. (2010). *Communication research strategies and resources* (10th ed.). Boston, MA: Wadsworth.

Schutz, D. E., Tannenbaum, S. I., & Lauterborn, R. F. (1998). *Integrated marketing communications: Putting it together and making it work.* Lincolnwood, IL: NTC Business Books.

Scott, W. (1955). Reliability of content analysis: The case of nominal scale coding. *Public Opinion Quarterly, 17*, 321–325.

Search Engine Optimization. (2009). Retrieved from http://en.wikipedia.org/wiki/Search_engine_optimization

Stacks, D. W. (2002). *Primer of public relations research*. New York, NY: Guilford.

Stacks, D. W. (Ed.). (2006). *Dictionary of public relations measurement and research*. Gainesville, FL: Institute for Public Relations. Retrieved from http://www.instituteforpr.org/ipr_info/dictionary_public_relations/

Stacks, D. W. (Ed.). (2007). *Dictionary of public relations research and measurement* (2nd ed.). Gainesville, FL: Institute for Public Relations. Retrieved from http://www.instituteforpr.org/ipr_info/dictionary_public_relations/

Stacks, D. W. (2010). *Primer of public relations research* (2nd ed.). New York, NY: Guilford.

Stacks, D. W., & Carroll, T. (2004). *Bibliography of public relations measurement*. Gainesville, FL: Institute for Public Relations. Retrieved from www.instituteforpr.org/research_single/bibliography_of_measurement/

Stacks, D. W., & Michaelson, D. (2004). *A pilot study of the "multiplier effect."* Paper presented at the Summit on Measurement, Durham, NH.

Stacks, D. W., & Michaelson, D. (2009). Exploring the comparative communications effectiveness of advertising and public relations: A replication and extension of prior experiments. *Public Relations Journal, 3*, 1–22. Retrieved from http://auth.iweb.prsa.org/xmembernet/main/pdfpull.cfm?prcfile=6D-030301.pdf

Stacks, D. W., & Salwen, M. B. (Eds.). (2009). *An integrated approach to communication theory and research* (2nd ed.). New York, NY: Rutledge.

Taylor, F. (1919). *The principles of scientific management*. New York, NY: Harper & Brothers.

Thurstone, L. L., & Chave, E. J. (1929). *The measurement of attitude*. Chicago, IL: University of Chicago Press.

Tinsley, H. E. A., & Weiss, D. J. (2000). Interrater reliability and agreement. In H. E. A. Tinsley & S. D. Brown (Eds.), *Handbook of applied multivariate statistics and mathematical modeling* (pp. 95–124). San Diego, CA: Academic Press.

Toth, E. L. (2009). *The future of excellence in public relations and communication management: Challenges for the next generation*. Mahwah, NJ: Lawrence Erlbaum.

U.S. Census Bureau. Retrieved from http://www.census.gov.

Waksberg, J. (1978). Sampling methods for random digit dialing. *Journal of the American Statistical Association, 73*, 40–46.

Weiner, M. (2007). *Unleashing the power of PR: A contrarian's guide to marketing and communication*. San Francisco, CA: International Association of Business Communicators.

Williams, F., & Monge, P. (2001). *Reasoning with statistics: How to read quantitative research* (5th ed.). Fort Worth, TX: Harcourt College Publishers.

Wright, D. W. (1990). Public relations research. Presentation made to the Chamber of Commerce, Jacksonville, FL.

Index

CPSIA information can be obtained at www.ICGtesting.com
Printed in the USA
BVOW020117080212

282395BV00003B/36/P